THE LADY OF TWO NATIONS

THE LADY OF TWO NATIONS

LIFE AND TIMES OF RA'ANA LIAQAT ALI KHAN

RAJ GOPAL SINGH VERMA

Published by
Renu Kaul Verma
Vitasta Publishing Pvt Ltd
2/15, Ansari Road, Daryaganj
New Delhi - 110 002
info@vitastapublishing.com

ISBN: 978-93-90961-26-9
© Raj Gopal Singh Verma
First Edition 2022
MRP ₹ 495

All Rights Reserved.
No part of this publication may be reproduced, stored in a retrieval system, or transmitted in any form, or by any means—electronic, mechanical, photocopying, recording or otherwise—without the prior permission of the publisher. Opinions expressed in this book are the author's own. The publisher is no way responsible for these.

Edited by Manjula Lal
Typeset & Cover Design by Somesh Kumar Mishra
Printed by Vikas Computer and Printers

To
all women who chart their own course

Contents

Foreword ix
Preface xiii

Tryst in Lucknow	1
A Conversion in 1871	12
Unexpected Proposal	32
And It Continues	38
On the Horns of a Dilemma	46
A Fateful Journey	52
Childish Pranks	58
Hurdles in Love	67
Nawab Saheb	76
Back Together	83
Together Forever	94
From Lucknow to Delhi	108
At Home with Jinnah	131

Mother, Wife and Policymaker	144
Famine, World War II and Transfer of Power	161
Towards Freedom	174
Flight to Fame	194
Suddenly Gone	213
Jinnah and Liaqat	225
Fatima and Ra'ana	230
After Liaqat	235
Diplomacy and Empowerment	242
Appendix	*255*
References	*257*

Foreword

Muslim women are often thought of as marginalised, excluded, discriminated against, and/or abused in Asian, African countries as well as in the Middle-East. News of Muslim women suffering abuse at the hands of religiously fanatic men give the impression that Muslim women have no agency or ability to resist this centuries old exploitation. Formal politics represent a theater that does not seem to allow any rights to Muslim women. The pleasant surprise is that Muslim-majority countries such as Kosovo, Kyrgyzstan, Senegal, Turkey, Indonesia, and in our neighbourhood Pakistan and Bangladesh have all had female political leaders at the highest levels of government.

The credit for political emancipation of Muslim women goes to Begum Ra'ana Liaquat Ali Khan who continued to remain active socially, politically and diplomatically, advancing the cause of the nascent state despite the gruesome political murder of her husband, Liaquat Ali Khan, first Prime Minister of Pakistan when she was barely 46 year old. The personality of this second-generation convert (From Kumaoni Brahmin to Christianity to Islam) is such that discussing her, one may end up pondering upon Pakistan and its issues coupled with their potential solutions. Her active participation in social and political life along mothering two teenaged son became a sort of model for other women aspirants in the Muslim country.

Though her marriage with a Muslim was between two semantic religions, the family of Ra'ana (Irene Pant) could not reconcile with this development. Little wonder, Nawabzada Liaqat Ali Khan could not visit his in-laws at Almora in Kumaon.

Raj Gopal Singh Verma preferred to join the profession of public relations, though his father, a veteran journalist Sh. Raj Roop Singh Verma was an editor and publisher of a popular Hindi daily from Muzaffarnagar. After earning a Bachelor Degree in Journalism from Mahrishi Dayanand University, Rohtak. Prof Tara Chand who interviewed him had been my teacher when I was pursuing the same course at Panjab University, Chandigarh. I enjoyed his affection so much that the only question he posed to Raj Gopal Singh Verma was "Do you know Anil Maheshwari?" Since then he did not turn back and is earning fame and name, a matter of pride for his friends.

Verma has meticulously weaved the incidents in the life of Ra'ana Liaquat Ali Khan in such an interesting way that the book becomes an engaging and engrossing read.

—**Anil Maheshwari,**
Author and Journalist
anil.ht@gmail.com

Preface

India, Pakistan and what is now Bangladesh, were part of united India before Partition of the sub-continent in 1947. Power structures in this vast country, first under the rule of the East India Company and then the British Crown were complex though it appeared a united land. Alien rulers like the Tughlaqs, Lodhis and Mughals exploited and robbed this land of its famed riches. Then came the British in the garb of traders, hiding their imperialist ambitions, who shrewdly eroded the harmonious atmosphere by sowing the seeds of communal and religious hatred among its heterogeneous population. The British so cleverly applied the policy of 'divide and rule' that a handful of their administrators were able to assert their superiority over millions of Indians.

World War II dealt a massive blow to break the political, economic and military might of the British Empire. This also caused intensification of anti-British discontent in India which reached such an extreme pitch that the European oppressors thought it in their interest to quit the country. Before leaving the shores, they not only partitioned the land into two independent countries but fragmented the territory in such a manner that people of different castes and religions looked upon one another with deep suspicion and distrust.

This is the story of Irene Sheela Pant, born in a tradition-bound Brahmin family that had converted to Christianity in such turbulent times. Her family's conversion, journey through the social and political terrain, and her marriage with a Muslim make for a sensational dramatic saga. By sheer chance, Irene happened to meet the son of the Nawab of Karnal and *jagirdar* of Muzaffarnagar, Liaqat Ali. He had just come back from Oxford after higher studies. It took little time for this brief encounter to metamorphose as though by magic, into eternal love.

Not much is known as to how, amid all the uncertainties and objections from Irene's family, their marriage took place. After the wedding, the bride came to be known by the name Gul-e-Ra'ana. Apart from fulfilling her role as Liaqat's life partner, she became the exclusive repository of his trust and a close associate. She was by his side through his political ascension. The thrill and success of that journey with her beloved husband form the central plot of this book, along with the adventures of the Kumaon belle who transformed from Irene to Begum Ra'ana.

Liaqat Ali was assassinated in 1951 at a time when he was holding the top post of the country. There is deep irony in the fact that one who possessed enormous wealth and authority in India and left everything for the cause of Pakistan would end up falling to an assassin's bullet. It is even more tragic that the purpose of this heinous murder has never been revealed. Under such trying circumstances, instead of allowing herself to breakdown, Ra'ana Begum marshaled her energies to plunge into meaningful social work, such as projects for organising and empowering women. Later, she was appointed ambassador to the Netherlands and Italy. During the reign of Zulfiqar Ali Bhutto, she was assigned charge of the Ministry of Finance in the Government of Pakistan. There she brought about several economic reforms in the ministry. When under the military dictatorship of Zia-ul-Haq, the deposed Prime Minister ZA Bhutto was hanged, Ra'ana Begum was the first to call it an act of political vendetta and mobilise a mass movement in open protest against it.

Dear to Jinnah as a daughter, Begum Ra'ana found a place in Pakistan's history waging a persistent fight against laws which were anti-women.

This book undertakes to narrate the eventful chronicle of this woman. References inevitably crop up to many contemporary political events in undivided India and Pakistan as without such context a proper portrayal of Begum Ra'ana would remain incomplete. Utmost care has been taken to maintain the authenticity of dates, historical occurrences and related facts, but imagination has also been allowed to play its role in filling the gaps. Nevertheless, there are many questions to which answers are yet to be found; for example, in the strained and often unpleasant relations between India and Pakistan, why Sheela Irene Pant alias Begum Ra'ana could not emerge as a notable figure to reduce this friction.

I was inspired by the suggestions proffered by my mentor Anil Maheshwari, whose visualisation and inspiration is manifested in this book. Besides, there were useful contributions of a richly informed historian, popularly known as the Pride of Agra, my writer friend, Raj Kishore Sharma 'Raje' who spent many wakeful nights in improving the manuscript, correcting its weaknesses and providing valuable suggestions. I sincerely express my gratitude to them.

Despite the care and caution, if any errors or other shortcomings are noticed, these may kindly be brought to my notice so that efforts can be made to improve them in forthcoming editions.

—**Raj Gopal Singh Verma**

Tryst in Lucknow

The radiant building of the Vidhan Sabha standing prominently on the main road of Lucknow is the city's finest attraction. Considered as one of the best examples of European architecture in the twentieth century, the facade of this semi-circular structure is built from the light brown sandstone quarried from Chunar near Mirzapur, located on the banks of the Ganga. In the centre of the crescent formation stands an umbrella-shaped canopy surrounded by numerous figures carved in stone. The summit of the triple-bow-shaped gateway is adorned by a royal emblem in marble. Exquisite, eye-catching paintings ornament numerous rooms, galleries and verandahs as well as the huge hall and beautifully curved flights of marble stairways.

This building was constructed by Samuel Swinton Jacob and Heera Singh while the foundation was laid by the then Governor, Spencer Harcourt Butler on 15 September 1922. The project was undertaken by Martin & Co. The prominent role played in the drawing of the blueprint and undertaking construction activities were assigned to Heera Singh. The imposing edifice was completed in the next five years and its formal opening took place on 21 February 1928.

A group of students of Lucknow University were given duty at the Legislative Assembly House to request people to buy tickets for a charity event to help flood-affected people of Bihar. Irene was among them, trying to reach a target of fund collection when she spotted a young politician. Intercepting him, she said, 'Excuse me, Sir! It is charity work...please, we need help...'

'All of a sudden? Like this? What help, ma'am? Don't you feel it is a little unusual?' The man appeared to be in a hurry, and so somewhat irritated, he prodded the young woman.

'Sir, don't be angry with me! I don't need anything for myself. A charity programme is being planned for the help of those rendered homeless in the Patna flood tragedy. You can come forward and show your generosity by buying one ticket for this programme.'

The young woman explained to him the ravages wreaked by the flood in Patna. The bright, young, fair-skinned young man looked quite debonair in his black suit and white shirt with a black-white striped tie. It was evident that he was under the influence of western culture while serving the people through politics. She felt it somewhat incongruent.

His eyes caught the small wad of tickets in her hand, and with an amused smile puckering up his mouth he said, 'Oh, so that is it… Of course, I have no objection to buying a ticket, ma'am!'

She looked pleased. 'Great! You are such a nice person; I must now change my opinion about you. You relieved me of my assignment. Shall I say thank you?'

'Oh, that's nothing! I haven't done anything remarkable. Please ask, if I can do anything for you'. Having said this in the well-bred gentlemanly manner, he put his hand in his pocket and began to rummage. Restlessly, the young woman remarked, 'In that case, you must purchase not one, but two tickets, Sir.'

Surprised at the audacity of the lady, the young man observed that there was no other person who was likely to accompany him to the show. Only one ticket would be sufficient. But the girl stood steadfast. She giggled, 'That's no reason, Sir. Bring someone along to give you company…and if that is not possible, tell me. Shall I get somebody to accompany you?'

Despite being so informal, she kept her gaze riveted to his eyes and added with a smile, 'Who wouldn't like to go with a person like you? It is my promise that if nothing happens, I shall offer myself to go along with you.'

When she, raising her big eyes to his amused ones, made this observation, the young man was left with no choice. He said, 'Undoubtedly, I'll take two tickets, and only you will give me company. Don't trouble yourself about finding anyone else.'

She tittered at this suggestion and said, 'Agreed, Sir! Hope that you will also find my commitment honoured!'

The promise was not something out of this world, as the young woman was anyhow supposed to be present at the show organised by her faculty, the Department of Sociology. How could she know that this brief encounter would turn her life along the path of unanticipated changes? It released that charming energy that would soon propel her into the magic world of new experiences and raise her to a different plane of existence.

The girl bid him goodbye and returned to her ticket-selling campaign. The young politician walked off.

The next day, for good reason, the young man was delayed. As it happened, the Governor had thrown a banquet at his residence in honour of the newly elected members of the Legislative Assembly. This appeared to eclipse the prospects of the gentleman joining the cultural programme.

Irene was to recite her poems in one of the sessions. She was busy preparing for it but, at the same time, her eyes were searching for someone special in the crowd. When a good part of the show was over, he arrived. Irene was yet to be called to the stage. She eagerly waved at him but he did not see her. Then she waded through the throng of people to reach him and welcoming him, expressed thanks that he made it to the programme.

He seemed interested in knowing her and enquired

about her studies and background.

'I'm Irene Sheela Margaret Pant, doing a Master's in Economics and Sociology', Irene offered by way of a formal introduction. He put his palms together in acknowledgement, saying, 'I'm Liaqat. I have a little interest in all subjects but very little in the subjects you're pursuing! I know a little Economics but yes, on the topics of Theology and Law, I can deal with everything!'

Liaqat delved deeper into their conversation.

'Sir, Law and Religion? Do you know that these subjects came into being much later? Since God created man he has always been looked upon as a social being. For ages, he went on roaming the earth in straggling herds, sometimes wandering in tribal groups, then over mountains, in jungles and stark wildernesses...his true identity as a human being formed through his pursuit of economic needs. That's why for me the two subjects are as important as the story of civilisation. Your Law and Religion, if I may honestly put it, invite a human being to follow the path of wily ways and deception and those who travel these roads are shown how to avoid the consequences of their deeds...'

Quite unbeknown to her, she was letting off a flood of wisdom that was overwhelming.

'That's all for the present, dear lady! Sometime when we meet, we'll discuss this a little more. Right now, this much will be enough!' Liaqat laughingly freed himself of this uncomfortable conversation.

'Oh, Sir! I'm ready too. Meanwhile, you should

keep your facts in order, so that when we have our next conversation, you won't feel uncomfortable! Let us wait for that next time...' She said in a and fearless manner.

'One thing intrigues me. If you don't mind, am I permitted to ask?' The way he put it, Irene could hardly have guessed what was coming. She simply said, 'Sure! Please ask.'

'Usually, we can get the idea of a person's caste and religion from his or her name, but in your case, it is simply not possible...Irene...Margaret...Sheela...and then Pant!' Liaqat put the puzzle before her.

'So, that's your problem! My full name is Sheela Irene Margaret Ruth Pant, Sir. But wouldn't it be comfortable if some facts and doubts remain a mystery so that the thrill is kept alive? If we come to know all today, wouldn't life be dull tomorrow, mister...?'

Laughing with youthful glee, she was trying to recall his name when he interposed to remind her, 'Liaqat.'

Nodding in affirmation, she tossed away the question. From a distance, a friend of hers was waving to her. It was time for her recitation. Abruptly, she rose to go.

Liaqat Ali Khan hailed from a Nawab family of Karnal. His father, the late Rukn-ud-Daula Shamsher Jang Nawab Rustum Ali Khan was the *jagirdar* of 300 villages of that region. Besides, he had also inherited a *jagir* covering half of the adjoining Muzaffarnagar district.

This family had come to India from Iran almost 500 years ago. The family members of Nawabs were recognised as descendants of the Emperor of Iran, Khusro

Nashirwan (531-78 AD). Liaqat got his early education at home and grew up into a talented and educated young man. Having completed graduation and law from the then Anglo-Oriental College which later came to be known as Aligarh Muslim University, he proceeded to Oxford University to pursue further studies. He obtained a Master's Degree in Law from there and was awarded the bronze medal. During his stay in Oxford, Liaqat took a keen interest in student politics and bagged the post of Honorary Treasurer of the students union. Later, at his professor's persuasion, he began practising law in London, but it was for a short period; a career in law was not the aim of young Liaqat.

Lucknow had become a well-developed city in the first half of the nineteenth century. European, Hindu and Muslim cultures vied with each other for a dominant position where Hindu cultural icons were trying to restore and regain their bygone era, the erstwhile Nawabs were waiting for some miracle to bring back Muslim splendour and magnificence. But the reins of power were firmly held by the British rulers even before 1857. However, it would be wrong to imagine that people's discontent with them had in any sense weakened.

It was during the First World War in 1915 that Mahatma Gandhi returned to India. He had an ambitious plan of mobilising the Indian people into a movement aimed at attaining freedom from the British Raj. In 1916, an important agreement was inked between the Congress Party and the Muslim League so that both would work jointly for the aim of self-rule. In this move that brought Hindus and Muslims together, Jinnah played a key role. At that time, he was called the 'ambassador of Hindu-Muslim unity'. This was followed by a few more significant developments such as the famous Champaran movement to improve the lot of farmers in Bihar, and formation of Kisan Sabha in Pratapgarh which offered a platform to the masses to launch effective resistance to the Britishers. The brutal incident of slaughter of the people at Jallianwalla Bagh in 1919 had stoked the fire of wrath in the populace and flared their passion to a greater intensity. By then, about 330 branches of Kisan Sabha had been set up all over the country which had its focus on the peasantry's discontent against the unjust rent law and *begari* (the practice of lowly paid labour), where poor farmers were being ruthlessly exploited. Mahatma Gandhi was also enraged over the savagery of the Jallianwala Bagh massacre and was aware of the outburst of anger all over the country. He advised people to exercise restraint while speaking at several public meetings at different places. He asked them to refrain from the use of violence and advised people to stick to peaceful resistance.

On the other hand, the Kakori Conspiracy Case had awakened the dormant sentiments of nationalists in the country. To give greater impetus to their movement, the revolutionaries needed money. Accordingly, a plot was hatched to attack the train carrying the government treasury on 9 August 1925. The Saharanpur-Lucknow passenger train which steamed off from Kakori station was force-stopped by pulling an emergency chain under the leadership of Pandit Ramprasad Bismil, Chandra Shekhar Azad, Ashfaqulla Khan and their associates. The train was assaulted and the government treasury was looted. The government took serious note of this incident and instituted cases against forty revolutionaries on charges of waging an armed struggle, looting the treasury and plotting to kill the passengers of the train. Rajendra Nath Lahiri, Pandit Ram Prasad Bismil, Ashfaqulla Khan and Thakur Roshan Singh were sentenced to death. Sixteen others were awarded either a minimum of four years imprisonment or maximum of a life term.

This proved to be a landmark incident, for it cast a deep effect on common peoples' thinking. The entire episode aroused a wave of political consciousness as had not occurred before, and sent tremors from one end of the land to the other. This consciousness gained greater momentum and strength in the ensuing days as was proved by incidents that coincidentally synchronised with the arrival of the Simon Commission. This Commission was appointed to bring about certain constitutional reforms, which in reality were nothing but a bag of tricks and deceptions, as it did not include a single Indian. This was enough reason to provoke nationwide protest marches. In Lucknow also students and youth came out in huge numbers in a display of their solidarity against the terms of Simon Commission and rent the air with slogans of 'Simon Go Back'.

Among this crowd was a girl of twenty-three years.

Wheat complexioned, possessing sharp features and watchful eyes, she was a short-statured student of Lucknow University. Originally belonging to Almora district of Kumaon, this young girl was known to be very intelligent from her childhood. She was bestowed with the talent of creating a place for herself wherever she went. Not only this, she was always at the top of her class and showed a maturity of understanding of political matters.

Despite utmost care and caution exercised by the British authorities, the walls of Lucknow soon became plastered with black and yellow slogans of 'Simon Go Back!'. By that time, the Secretariat of the United Provinces had been shifted from Allahabad to Lucknow and with that came Daniel Pant. Pant's children were growing into adolescence; of them, the daughter got admission in the postgraduate programme in the university and the son Norman got into the local Christian College. He too, like his elder sister, was attracted to the fight for freedom. Norman began to take part in activities whose aim was to free the country from British rule.

In those days of political upsurge, Motilal Nehru and Jawaharlal Nehru used to address mass meetings in Lucknow's Aminabad Park, exhorting the youth to openly participate in the freedom struggle. A few other interesting ways of opposing the Simon Commission were devised by some sections of the people. Amusingly, some of them floated black kites in the sky when the *taluqdars* of Awadh hosted a tea party in honour of Sir John Simon, while a few others released black kites above and over the party.

That was the year when devastating floods occurred in the city of Patna. As per revenue records, Odisha was part of Bihar then, but the British government was least concerned about people's safety. The Sociology Department of Lucknow University had thus organised a cultural programme to help the flood-affected areas, for which students were asked to collect funds.

Patna and water are bound in an inseparable relationship. This city is situated on the southern bank of the river Ganga and northern bank of the river Punpun. Ganga runs parallel in a straight line alongside Patna; the city is enclosed on three sides by Ganga, Punpun and Sone rivers. Hajipur falls in the North of Patna where the river Gandak joins the Ganga. In the days of the British, Patna began to expand westwards and had joined Danapur in a steady spread. Considering these facts, it is not surprising that Patna frequently faces the fury of floods.

A Conversion in 1871

The family backgrounds of Liaqat Ali Khan and Irene were quite distinct. In the breath-takingly beautiful surroundings of Almora, amid natural vistas of earthly paradise so popular with tourists, Irene was born in a Brahmin family of these Kumaon areas. Like her grandfather Tara Dutt Pant, she was also known as a little out-of-the ordinary by temperament. There was a time when his fame had a meteoric rise as an accomplished and expert *Vaidya* (Ayurvedic doctor). His profound knowledge of herbs and their therapeutic properties and his treatment skills proved such an asset that his name travelled far beyond the high hills of Almora to every unthinkable remote place.

For another and an altogether different reason, he

became famous in the year 1871. It became the talk of the town in Nainital and soon spread to adjoining areas that staunch Brahmin Tara Dutt Pant has relinquished his religion and chosen to convert to Christianity.

It is inconceivable to think that this piece of news would not kick up a big row all over Almora and the neighbouring district Nainital. It reverberated through narrow alleys and streets of the hill stations, creating waves of anger and hatred which were very offensive. Re-telling it in today's times may sound unbelievable, but bonds of caste and clan were not just a matter of personal importance and status—they were considered society's responsibility and a question of honour for the whole community. If a responsible Brahmin family behaved in this manner, what message would it convey to others? Unimaginable! A conflagration flared up in no time and demonstrations and protest rallies against Tara Dutt Pant took place, no less in intensity than what people were used to seeing against the British rule. Slogan-shouting mobs assembled and pelted stones at the family mansion.

Pant families had settled in villages such as Uproda, ChuntJajoot, and Khantali. The Pants in question lived in Gangolihat which was called Brahmapuri (the city of Brahmins). The decision to adopt Christianity had made such an impact on staunch believers in the age-old traditions of Kumaon that they felt betrayed and broken. They feared that this would lead to further weakening of their respectable position, casting long shadows on the younger generation. They began to worry about protecting themselves against possible contamination. People were already blaming the English for intruding on their lands to capture their traditional holdings and destroying their professions; now the fear loomed large of a greater and far more dangerous menace in the form of the English subverting their sacred faith and sacraments and annihilating all that came to them as divine blessings and benediction.

In any case, British and American missionaries had been active in the hills winning local people's trust and gaining success in their campaign, but this success was more than what they might have hoped for. Their hold was seen only on those who belonged to the bottom rung of the social strata—the labour class, orphans and the abandoned, destitute, widowed or discarded women, physically challenged, the illiterate and their children. Such people could easily be brought under the Christian umbrella. Their social position was almost nil and it mattered little when they left their original Hindu faith and adopted Christianity. That is why such occurrences at the lowest level did not constitute any recognisable danger to the settled Hindu society.

The case of Tara Dutt Pant was quite different. The first thought that came to the people was that it represented a serious threat to Kumaon's culture. This was a culture that for centuries the adherents of the Pant community believed it their holy duty to safeguard and conserve. And now one of their respectable family heads was discarding it as casually as though it was a most common act of day-to-day life. To adopt as one's own a religion whose British followers came to this country to capture by brutal force and in an unconstitutional manner, using crude methods of physical violence, was an act that could not easily be countenanced. It was quite natural that this development provoked extensive protests. The belief that if such incidents were not checked in time, they were bound to erode the foundations of traditional society, stirred in everyone the impulse to take urgent action.

Tara Dutt Pant's conversion had taken place in Benaras (Varanasi) and his return to Almora created a veritable storm in this tranquil place. Angry crowds demanded an explanation from him and put pressure on him to declare his faith in the Hindu religion. But Tara Dutt had not taken this step in haste or unthinkingly. High British officials had been fully informed about it. Lieutenant Governor of the United Provinces Sir William Muir and Commissioner of Kumaon Sir Henry Ramsay came forward to offer assistance. These authorities convinced this well-known personage of the Pant clan to agree to acquaint the restless crowd with his decision and his line of thinking in an address to them. Tara Dutt Pant made his speech in such a decorous and disciplined manner that it compelled most of them to accept his arguments quietly; those who had been more bellicose turned disinterested.

On the surface, to the world, both the British officers had succeeded in quelling the fire of discontent with their farsightedness, but the embers were still smouldering.

Nobody knew how long this question would agitate the minds of the people and when its after-effects would be felt. It was not a question of a single family but involved the whole Pant community—in the long run, the entire hilly population and the religious structure of faith received a blow, making people question themselves. When it comes to society, it appears inevitable that all close ranks and stand united.

This case was no different. Orthodox and conservative segments joined hands in persuading Tara Dutt to come back to the Brahmanical fold and Hindu faith, their efforts persisting to the last. But when it became clear that nothing could dissuade him, the diehard Hindus struck an alternative plan, to resort to harassment and create humiliating difficulties for him.

Under pressure from the upper-class people, close friends and relatives of Tara Dutt openly proclaimed severance of their relationship with the errant family. He was declared '*Ghata Shraddh*' which indicated that the community felt that they held no kind of relationship with this family and considered it as good as non-existent. Members of the family were debarred from visiting others of their caste and also from attending any function or celebration of bereavement or ritual of auspicious nature from that point of time. In short, they were as good as dead for others in this land of their birth.

The scattered societies of the hilly terrain of Kumaon are marked by the preponderance of certain caste systems and their role in maintaining them. General mass psyche here is deeply rooted in age-old customs and practices which assert their power unquestioned. Following the ancient *Varna* system, Char Chothani Brahmins wield the central authority. To demonstrate their importance and high status, they had been granted the privilege to wear their *dhoti* down to the ankle and heavy gold jewellery. Besides, they enjoyed many other privileges. They were not only exempt from tax payment, but were protected against punishment for criminal offences, even to the extent that if one of this caste committed a murder, he couldn't be sentenced to death but might have to serve a life term. They were supposed to be engaged in intellectual and mental activities and not do any kind of physical work.

Somewhat beneath this stratum were the Brahmins of lower order who were allowed to wear only silver and copper ornaments—not those of gold. A short *dhoti* and a blanket or a sheet were thrown over the shoulders, defining their lower status in the hierarchy. Some of them worked on their farms and fields and so came to be called *haldhar* (plough-wielding) Brahmins.

For a member of the long *dhoti*-wearing Pant sect to abandon his fold to join a new religion was considered not only an audacious act connoting defiance, but a cruel assault on the orthodoxies of a well-entrenched faith which offered a challenge to all. People felt that a deep wound had been inflicted on their sentiments, giving room for all kinds of unchecked gossip and rumours in the wake of such a turn of events.

Tara Dutt Pant was the son of Pandit Hari Ram Pant and was born in a place called Jait. Recognising his father's expertise in medicine, the royal family of Nepal invited him to their court and offered him the post of royal *Vaidya*. It is believed that in 1859, when the British were grappling with the after-effects of the country's first armed revolt which they called Sepoy Mutiny and were seeking to consolidate their power, Pandit Hari Ram decided to settle down in Kathmandu. It is here that he began to impart the scientific knowledge of *Vaidya Shastra* to his grown son.

Young Tara Dutt grew up watching his father visit dense Himalayan forests to collect a variety of medicinal herbs and compound them into different drugs and medicines. Proximity with his gifted father made it fairly easy for Tara Dutt to imbibe the difficult and complex knowledge of traditional Indian medicine and his fame as a cure provider spread far and wide.

Pandit Hari Ram Pant had begun his search for a suitable bride for his son from Kumaon. In the same year, Tara Dutt got married to Durga Joshi who hailed from a respected family in Almora. Her father was Diwan or Prime Minister of the Kumaon state. It is believed that this marriage opened the gates of good luck for both. Tara Dutt had already acquired considerable fame as an effective *Vaidya*, at the same time he began showing extraordinary genius in *Dharma Shastra* (Theology). He was often found immersed in the study of volumes on the subject and showed a burning urge to participate in high-level polemics and discussions whenever such occasions presented themselves.

This was noted by the royal family, who offered all possible assistance and encouragement to him. In those days, Benaras used to be favoured as the most suitable place for religious discourses and grand polemical debates of this kind. His father Hari Ram decided to take his son to Benaras to further refine and improve his scholarly inclination. The result was that Tara Dutt acquired such depth of knowledge and sharpness in the subject matter that with amazing facility he was able to vanquish his opponents.

It is considered that extensive foraging in ancient books and treasure troves of knowledge produced such a desire for an assiduous quest that later on it became a source of alienation. But in those days no one could tell what was hidden in the unknown depths of the future.

While in Benaras, he came under the influence of the prosperous Chitpavan Brahmin, Neelkant Shastri, who was born in 1825 and had been settled permanently in Benaras. He was exceptionally talented in debating and was a fearless scholar, never withdrawing from any serious discussion which offered a challenge to established theological precepts and doctrines. Those were times when Christian missionaries were fully engaged in strengthening their hold and since Benaras had become the centre of spiritual and religious scholarships, the Christians there found themselves in perpetual conflict with local sages and scholars. In such a charged atmosphere,

Neelkant Shastri offered an invitation to one missionary named William Smith to resolve through debate which religion was superior—Hinduism or Christianity. Clever Williams went on avoiding the debate. Whenever the question was raised, William would advise Shastri to first peruse the Holy Bible thoroughly.

Neelkant Shastri spent three years simply studying the Bible. The unexpected outcome of his labours of these three years was that he discarded the Hindu mantle and adopted Christianity in 1848. He formed a new religion, named it 'Nemia' and closely studied the strengths and weaknesses of all religions. He began imparting theological knowledge, gave lessons and went for a tour of England, though what he saw there with his own eyes was disappointing.

Tara Dutt had already come under the spell of Episcopal masters; now establishing contact with them, he began the study of the Bible in right earnest. After a long period of dilemma, Tara Dutt took the momentous decision which was to leave a deep and lasting impression on the future course of his life and his family's fortune. In 1871, he was admitted into Christianity, formally baptised and given the name of Joshia. On April 25 of the same year, his wife and daughters too got converted.

Pant had three daughters who were christened Ruth, Lydia and Imogene in that order. His mother's inner conflict can easily be imagined. She must have suffered a great deal of internal tug-of-war with her conscience, but to face the insurmountable opposition of her relatives—

now turned hostile, neighbours, her caste and the entire society was no small agony. For her, it was a life-long war against all the visible and invisible forces that were determinedly united in their bitter antagonism to this impetuous family. During those stormy days of switching over to the other religion, Durga was with child, whose was eagerly awaited by everyone. On 11 July, following the birth of three daughters, the birth of a son brought immense joy to everyone in the family. The child was named Daniel Devidutt.

Meanwhile, Tara Dutt decided to go to Lahore to get educated in Christian Theology. Lahore's Theological College was recognised as a premier centre for such education. But he had to cut short his stay and return, as his daughter Ruth was seriously ill. While he was carrying her to Almora, great disaster befell him. The anger of the people against this family's conversion became serious and spread widely. It also took a violent turn. Tara Dutt was not only exorcised from the community but declared dead to the world. He was deprived of his share in the family property and his name was struck off from joint heritage land holdings, though it is also a fact that the Pastor of Budden Church, John Henry Budden who was an official of the London Missionary Society, tried to help him as much as he could. He sold to this hapless man a small plot of land close to the church where Tara Dutt later constructed a house. When he came to Almora, Christian missionaries had consolidated their position by doing a good deal of work. Henry Ramsay had assumed the office of Commissioner of Kumaon division and appeared friendly to the church. He gave all indication of co-operation towards it and its activities, especially towards those who faced hostile boycott and other forms of harassment from the local populace owing to their conversion. Christian missionaries considered it their duty to provide material facilities like land or house to the banished Hindus and help them lead an honourable life in a friendly society. Such uprooted and converted people were settled in a place in Almora called Heera Dungri, whereas in Pithoragarh the locality of converted people was called Bhatcot.

Haunted by these inclement circumstances, Pant summoned the courage to make a new beginning. In Benaras, he had already been informed of the dire consequences of what he was doing but imagining what those 'dire consequences' would be was not as painful as actually experiencing them. It was quite horrifying to face the actual fury of large numbers of his community and town. He found himself in the centre of a storm when he returned. At every step, his strength and stamina were being tested; on one hand, he was trying to assimilate in the Christian society, on the other, he felt the curse of being insulted, humiliated, jeered, booed and heckled in the street. Even those whom he regarded his close friends now turned their backs on him or just vanished when they saw him coming. He was neither invited to any social gathering nor could he think of being invited to one. Worse was the case of Durga, now baptised as Sarah. But she did not accept defeat. It is said that gradually and with quiet perseverance, she was successful in restoring some sort of close contacts with some of her relations. From her mother's side, small gifts and tokens of affection kept coming and it is also said that her son Daniel was permitted by the neighbours to watch the proceedings of the Brahmanical function 'Bagwali' and even participate in it.

Daniel's parents and sisters had to bring about basic changes in their day-to-day activities and lifestyle. For instance, instead of performing the ritual *puja* before partaking of meals, they began their day with prayers in the Christian tradition. In place of evening prayers, they read the Bible before going to bed. There was neither any seasonal fast as usually happens in a Hindu family, nor did they feel any excitement about the approaching Hindu festivals. All the big and small festivals lost meaning and relevance in their lives. The holy thread (*janeu*) was given up, so was the sacred sandalwood paste mark on the forehead or the vermilion dot.

As for dressing style, neither Tara Dutt's family nor any other in similar conditions effected any change in the clothes they wore. Women-folk still donned traditional long skirts called *ghaghra* and bodice. However, some slight novelty was discerned in men's style. The hat or western cap crept slowly into their fashion consciousness. One of the prominent questions in this changed perspective was that of adjusting with others who had also got converted to Christianity. They mostly comprised people from lower castes of Hindu society considered inferior to the status the Pants enjoyed. Given this cultural disparity, it was not an easy matter to live at par with them, for the feeling of caste superiority and consideration of hierarchy didn't just vanish with conversion! But for Tara Dutt, this issue didn't come in the way of comfortably settling down among these new neighbours because of his medical practice. Besides he was himself lenient and adjustable and didn't follow the strict precepts and rules the *Varna* system had been enjoining upon his caste. He found it easy to gain people's confidence through his affable, genial nature.

Tara Dutt's second daughter Harpriya Lydia also cherished a desire to enter the medical profession, but not the Ayurvedic tradition. She wished to pursue modern medicine. It is to her credit that she completed her education from Agra Medical College and felt that greater opportunities awaited her.

She earned the distinction of being one of the few select women to obtain formal qualification from the Royal College of Physicians and the Royal College of Surgery. Queen Victoria conferred on her special honours for standing up bravely as a woman in a male-dominated profession and accomplishing such high distinction. Lydia had the option to stay back in England and practice but she elected to come back to her country and dedicated herself to the good of its people. She began by working in Mission Hospital, Almora and then in Faizabad. Lydia didn't marry, perhaps owing to the complex conditions stemming from religious issues. It wasn't really easy to get good matches in the Christian community in those days.

Her brother Daniel Devidutt Pant initially studied in Almora. Later, he also went to Lucknow for further studies and afterwards got selected for a post in the Public Works Department. Daniel got married on 15 March 1901 to Annie Margaret alias Mohini Singh in the Methodist Indian Church at Lucknow.

Irene was born in 1905 in Almora. Her name derives from the Greek word which means 'peace', being also the name of the Greek Goddess of Peace (spelt as Eirene). Daniel had to spend his time in three different places—Allahabad, Lucknow and Nainital—in connection with his job. His posting was in Allahabad but he was accustomed to spending six months a year in Nainital, where the Methodist Church ran Wellesley High School. This facilitated his offsprings' education in a reputed school. In due course, Irene also got enrolled there with her elder sister Shanti as a day scholar. Irene became exceptionally popular among her teachers as well as her schoolmates for her sharp, smart mind. She had a strong appeal because of her prominently expressive eyes and beautiful face. About her, the father wrote these words briefly in his diary:

'She got a good name as a pupil in kindergarten. Her teachers regarded her as a very intelligent student.'

Irene's mother took a keen interest in preparing her children for school, which gave her a sense of satisfaction and joy. Once when Irene went to school wearing her mother's favourite red apparel, her teachers called her 'Red Riding Hood'. She spent three memorable years in the school during which she learnt a lot. Music was one of her hobbies. She was gifted with a good voice and surprised everyone when she played the piano or strummed the guitar. Later, she tried to inculcate these qualities in her kids too.

Irene and her sisters invariably faced one serious problem. Nainital being the summer capital, government officers used to halt there for six months and afterwards move to Allahabad or Lucknow. This naturally created an inconvenient interruption in their studies. Daniel and Annie got more and more worried about their budding daughters. Ultimately, they agreed to get them admitted in Lucknow's Lal Bagh Boarding School. Irene got into the fifth class of this missionary school, founded by one American Methodist Christian, Isabella Thoburn.

In 1870, Isabella Thoburn started a school with just six girls, then located in Aminabad Bazaar. She was passionate about women's education and devotedly worked for it. The school was shifted in 1871 to its building in Lal Bagh which was one of the rich possessions of the last Nawab of Awadh. The magnificence and grandeur of this red brick building with its crenellated walls and exquisitely shaped high arches reflected the aristocratic culture in which it was built. Among Indian Christians, it held a prestigious place of being the centre of exclusive education.

Thereon came a problem. Irene had studied in the

European type of school in Nainital where the medium of teaching was English, and the Lal Bagh School, catering to children from diverse backgrounds, used the prevalent Hindustani-Urdu medium. Acknowledging popular sentiment, the British administration recognised it as an official language. After some initial difficulties, Irene and her sister not only became proficient in the language but proved their talent by racing ahead of others.

It must have hardly taken one year for Irene to master the subtleties and fine nuances of a different kind of Urdu in this all-girls school, which made her teachers wonder at the girls' ability to learn and attain proficiency in an alien script in just one year. This produced two results. One, she was always at the forefront in studies, and two, she found it far easier to adapt to the culture of Lucknow, which was so different from Almora. It was because of her superior grasp of Urdu that she got top marks. No doubt, this facility with the language stood her in good stead as the wife of the first Prime Minister of Pakistan.

It is common knowledge that though the aristocratic Nawabi culture may not have done much to improve the condition of common people, its contribution towards enriching a distinct life of refined tastes and habits remains unrivalled. The capital of Awadh was shifted from Faizabad to Lucknow during the declining period of the Mughal rule. There is little doubt that the arrival of the East India Company saw decay of this Nawabi culture, with Nawab Wajid Ali Shah's vast possessions having been captured by the British and his having been exiled to Calcutta (now Kolkata). But even today, the city's beautiful gardens and orchards and the radiant splendour of its palatial buildings are as vibrant as they were in their prime. Especially notable is the peculiar hold the Urdu language has on the minds and hearts of Lucknow's citizens which, despite the rapid escalation of English, co-extensive with the strengthening of the English rule, continued to increase. This enchanted submission of the people to the charms of the language didn't seem to diminish over time. The fine aspects of Lucknow's charming social manners and etiquette result from a highly refined Muslim culture, which is exemplified in the adage of '*Pehle aap!*' (You first!)

In an age when a girl absorbs all the intricate influences that she is exposed to, Irene also quickly imbibed the culture of courtesy, sophisticated responses and the chiselled roundedness of the elite Muslim society. Having finished school, Irene took admission in Isabella Thoburn College for higher studies. Once, a professor in a college programme declared from the podium:

> Wherever she is, one can expect liveliness and activity. To have such an agile student full of zest for life is a matter of both joy and great responsibility.
>
> There is no doubt Irene was born with extraordinary talent and intelligence, and Lucknow's culture left a deep impression on her permanently. In shaping it, her family struggled hard against unexpected adversities, some of which we have

already mentioned. She was by nature a generous woman. She used to take a deep interest in social work, harbouring special consideration for those who urgently needed help and succour. Those were times when a woman was not supposed to step out of home, as society frowned upon such free movement. Irene, however, did not care for these sanctions and always took steps that defied social tolerance and acceptability. She did not value these traditional restrictions when it came to offering assistance to the needy and poured her heart and soul into working for them.

Had Irene's mother not supported her, perhaps this young woman would have had to restrain her zeal and keep more or less to herself. But Annie herself possessed a charitable temper which seems to have passed on to her daughter. She always took time out to pay attention to the needy families of Almora, even though society in one voice had imposed grave sanctions on this family for their intransigence.

In her spare time, she would visit the sanatorium in the neighbouring Falsimi village and work for the patients. Whenever time permitted, Irene also went along to assist her. Annie's social work was limited to not just this kind of service: If she came to know that some family was facing dire financial problems, she would prepare meals for them and supply other essentials without wasting time. The hearts of the suffering people would brim over with gratitude for the noble selfless sentiments and compassion with which the mother-daughter team worked to provide them comfort.

Annie's family had come from Nepal and settled in India as a rehabilitated family. They had gone through untold hardships which left painful memories etched in their minds. The horrors of those days had been tucked away in some corner of their minds. But it also enabled Annie to empathise with the deprived and destitute people who had nobody to look up to. For such people, she emerged as god-sent, showing noble qualities of dedication and readiness to suffer in order to alleviate their suffering. The then Governor conferred a certificate of appreciation for her work. Whenever Irene's commitment to charity work was lauded, she made a special mention of her mother's inspiring life as the real motivational force.

By the time Irene was ready to go to college, political developments in India and particularly in Lucknow, had turned tense and quite volatile. In the beginning, Indians tried to cooperate with the British as much as possible. For instance, in World War I, Indian soldiers fought on the side of the British and laid down their lives in large numbers. But their sacrifices mostly went unsung and unacknowledged.

The British treated the large-scale deaths in the war and consequently the destitution of their families in India with something amounting to inhuman apathy or contempt. The grief was further exacerbated by their levying extra taxes on the poor in a bid to prop up the rapidly depleting coffers of the government. It is not difficult to see how angry and disillusioned people had become, for they came out in great numbers protesting against the shabby manner in which they were being treated.

Unexpected Proposal

A beautiful woman in a *sharara* and *salwar* was sitting at a table in the isolated corner of Wenger's Café from where she could conveniently observe the movement of visitors. The Confectionary and Café shop was agog with plenty of bustle, but this lady was waiting for someone special, which is why she looked so listless. Ignoring the rich aroma of a combination of delicacies, she kept raising her eyes in the direction of the glass panel door of the entrance and appeared to be trying to look past it, again and again. This grand Café used to be the regular and most preferred haunt of British officers, Nawabs and the who's who of elite society. And why not? The place had become the most known spot for its exclusive preparations, so delicious, and so tasty!

'Hello!'

Voila! There he was. Finally. Half rising, bowing a little in the comeliest manner, the young lady greeted the man for whom she had been consulting her wristwatch sometimes and sometimes peering through the windows and the door.

'Good day, Irene! Beg to be excused for being a little late.'

The middle-aged man pulled his chair a little closer while expressing his regret for the delay. Was he late? Maybe, maybe not! Yes, primarily because he was much elder to Irene Margaret Pant—by nearly ten years; secondly, he was already married; and thirdly, he was a Muslim.

On the other hand, there were strong reasons for 'No' as well. One, it was well known that he was numbered among the frontliners of nationalist freedom fighters with strength and resolve that made him stand out prominently; two, he had been educated in Oxford University; three, and this strongly went in his favour, he hailed from the reputed and noble Nawab family of Karnal and Muzaffarnagar. Their *jagir* seemed to stretch endlessly everywhere. In 1926, adding another feather to his cap, he got elected to the United Provinces Assembly from Muzaffarnagar Muslim constituency.

In their first meeting in the cultural programme at Lucknow, they came to know one another's views in some vague way. She was a Christian but her ancestors were Brahmins who had later converted to Christianity. Her father Daniel Pant was employed as an officer in the Secretariat under the British administration and got postings in Lucknow and Nainital. Irene herself manifested frankly liberal opinions and had been educated in Isabella Thoburn College under Lucknow University for her Master's in Economics and Sociology. She was interested in Financial Management, but also had a good command over other subjects, especially the subject of women's empowerment, international affairs and diplomacy.

Their first meeting was casual and could easily have been forgotten had this Nawab not made it into headlines as the fond topic of public discussion for his powerful deliberations from numerous fora. By this time, Irene had become a lecturer in Economics in Delhi's Indraprastha College. She lived there with a friend.

Liaqat Ali Khan's impressive speech on the Simon Commission in the Assembly sent great waves not only through Lucknow but all the way to Delhi and most of the cities of North India. It figured prominently in the newspapers and came to be seen not only as a fine specimen of expression of ideas but as articulating a Muslim youth's views who had come to represent every Indian's thoughts about participatory rule. It was, therefore, not at all surprising that Liaqat Ali was soon flooded with congratulatory letters from all corners.

That evening, when Irene returned to her room in the Girls' Friendly Society Women Hostel, her room partner Christina smiled and said, 'Did you read today's newspaper, Irene?'

'No, not as yet.'

Irene sprinkled some water on her face and while wiping it, answered.

'Take it, then. Read. It's in the second main headline. You know Liaqat, anyway... Now he has become the Deputy Leader of the United Provinces Assembly. You can at least send him greetings. His election and speech both, are hot topics of discussions.'

'But I hardly know him. That meeting was just a short one for a few minutes. And now he is a tall leader... He wouldn't even recall me!'

'Are you so forgettable? Besides, it's common courtesy. Everyone likes to be remembered at these important times.'

Christina tried to instill some confidence in her in a somewhat teasing manner. Ultimately, Irene agreed to write a four-line letter of congratulations to Liaqat. She conveyed her greetings and also informed him of her job in Delhi.

Having posted it, she forgot about the matter. But it appears that the Nawab had not forgotten her. One evening she was surprised to get a sealed envelope on her return from college. Her heart fluttered madly when her eyes fell on the sender's name and address. On her way to her room on the first floor, she opened the envelope mid-way on the staircase and read the epistle to the end. It was written in English and read as follows:

> Dear Irene,
>
> Thanks for your greetings.
>
> Lucky I am that you thought me worthy of your

consideration. Good news is that you're in Delhi which is located at an equal distance from Karnal and Muzaffarnagar. This will make me visit the place quite often. Next Saturday I may halt for some time in Delhi while coming from Lucknow. If you can spare some time, could we have a cup of coffee at Wenger's Bakery in Connaught Place? I shall be there exactly at thirty minutes past five in the evening.

– Liaqat

Despite the cool weather, drops of perspiration emerged on Irene's forehead as she finished the letter. A delicious feeling of thrill and curiosity coursed through her and suffused her consciousness. She anxiously waited for Christina, with whom she intended to share it.

The appointed day dawned. Irene was firm about taking Christina with her but the latter said, 'Nothing doing! Matters of sentiment must be talked over only between the two. Don't take it as a childish thing; it is a serious matter, dear.'

'No...no...it's not a matter of the heart...one of a light-hearted amusement!'

It was Irene who tried to put things in the right perspective. In reality, Irene could not convince herself that Liaqat was in any sense serious about the meeting and desired to meet her in earnest—though he did not just express his wish but actually fixed a date and time.

She didn't know in what direction this rendezvous

would take her. The day was Saturday and it was the second Saturday of the month. College was scheduled to be closed that day.

And It Continues

'How long have you been waiting?'

When Liaqat said this in a rather formal manner, Irene also responded in a matching tone and words, 'Just now. You aren't so late. Don't you worry. It wouldn't matter even if you were late. My college is "off" today. You are coming from out of town, your being late can be excused.'

She laughed, and Nawab Liaqat gently smiled in a somewhat informal manner.

'What would you like to have?' He asked, to which she replied, 'Whatever you choose to order.'

'Two piping hot coffees with froth and a little chocolate spread' was the order placed. When the Nawab mentioned that the pastry of this place enjoyed the reputation of perfect taste, Irene couldn't restrain herself. It was clear that both had a sweet tooth.

Then the scope of this informal and unusual meeting unfolded. The topics ranged from Karnal, Muzaffarnagar and went on to cover Delhi, Lucknow, British Raj, India's future and even touched upon international concerns! Discussions became more and more lively as they chatted about the country's economic condition, the ruinous role of East India Company, the 1857 Sepoy Mutiny and current developments. Liaqat expressed his opinion in no uncertain terms:

'The British will have to leave this country. We must shrug them off mentally. Leaving aside the religious, communal and caste-related beliefs we must become progressive…But are we ready? This country is not made up of just two communities. It has a common shared legacy, who knows how ancient! The saddest part is that our caste and religious affinities have worked like termites in nibbling the country's economic system and culture completely hollow. They are aliens and traders to boot. Why should we watch this legacy getting destroyed right before our eyes? We have been wasting our energies in irrelevant issues of communal and religious controversies which only help the rulers. Even now, it is not too late: We can wake up and seize the opportunity to stir the masses. This is the only way we can prepare the next generation, which will be strong and broad-minded; the generation which, I feel, is drifting away from us.'

Irene had no differences of opinion on these broad

points. Rather, she was in close agreement with what he said. She had also been preparing a blueprint for bringing the country's economy back on track, for which Liaqat had offered her ample encouragement. He wanted to make her a member of the core committee which would be given the task of preparing an economic blueprint for the independent India of his dreams, a self-reliant India which she had been desiring with all her heart. But there remained some questions begging for answers. And they must wait for those answers.

At last, the time came for them to part. He was so impressed with her knowledge and point of view that he did not even realise that she had made her way into his mind and heart. Before he said goodbye, Liaqat Ali fixed the next rendezvous with her at Delhi's Chelmsford Club. Irene's roommate Christina was also invited to the dinner.

Liaqat then headed to Karnal, from there he was scheduled to visit his constituency Muzaffarnagar, where he had a residence. Although Irene was ten years younger than him, her ideas offered promise of a bright future, even if it were two decades ahead. Now and then her opinions and images would hover in his mind which forced his thoughts to the difficult point: 'To be or not to be.'

The following week, when he came to Delhi again and welcomed his lovely guest, his heart dictated a decision to his mind. He wished to tie the knot with Irene. He needed a life partner who would work in close unison with him and walk alongside step by step in his quest for achieving social and political goals, and thus complete the circle that remained still imperfect and incomplete.

The Nawab arrived well in time at this exclusive club reserved only for the privileged few at Lutyens Delhi, proudly standing at Raisina Marg. Irene was asked to come at seven, but the impatient suitor was present half an hour before. This handsome and sober gentleman, now in typical Indian Muslim *sherwani* and *achkan,* must have seen many a cultural hue and shade in this world before reaching here today. Irene herself was drawn to his frank and easy nature which sparkled like a gem with his rarefied cultural manner—accounted for the same tug of attraction that Liaqat felt. Moreover, she was at an age when a person does not give serious thought to factors like religion, nor cares for age or the value of status if other things impress her. He or she probes only the heart. Each of them had taken a measure of the other to the point of satisfaction. But it is also true that in that initial stage, Irene did not succeed in getting a glimmer of love in her probing of the Nawab's heart.

The Chelmsford Club was a famous meeting place in British Delhi which admitted only highly placed officers, top bureaucrats and their family members, the nobility and the royalty, and chosen privileged businessmen. It had started functioning only three years back, in 1928, though it was conceived in 1917. It offered all means of luxurious recreation contrived by the wealthy class for its leisure-time amusement as an ostensible display of its place in society and provided the satisfaction of belonging to it. The Club had a top-class lawn tennis court, billiard and card rooms, squash courts, bar and café for the elite gentry to spend their vast leisure hours.

That day a doorman was specially posted at the gate of the club under strict instructions to take particular care of two distinguished young lady guests and escort them to the table. When he came to the table escorting the two ladies, the Nawab glanced at his wristwatch, which was ticking at 7.22 pm.

'Welcome, ladies! So, the score is even, eh?'

Liaqat's remarks seemed to provoke even the subdued lights and music to an uncontrolled burst of joy and laughter.

'For you Nawab Saheb, life is pretty simple—just put on a *sherwani*, then *achkan*, comb your hair…that's that! Ask us women, what an intricate web of motions of preparing oneself it demands! If we ever took it into our heads to step out just as we are, even our families would decline to recognise us.'

Christina said this with such unconscious *naiveté* that for a long time the air kept quivering with laughter.

'Let us keep a plethora of complaints for later, first let us introduce ourselves. Please meet Christina, my bosom pal, my confidant, in whom half of my heart beats…And you, *huzoor,* Nawab Liaqat Ali Saheb, who is seen more in the newspaper headlines than face to face.'

Irene's eyes sparkled with runaway emotions and a naturally blossoming smile moved over her lips as she did the introductions. Liaqat gracefully acknowledged it with due courtesy, bowing a little as per the etiquette of his class.

'My great fortune! Thanks for such elevating words', he said.

The conversation at once picked up a good pace as on both sides there flowed gurgling talk. The fact that they had recently met helped them become informal in no time. It was surprising that despite being a reserved person, Liaqat found it not at all hard to gather the courage he required to reveal to her his heart's desire! Who knows, tomorrow it might be just too late!

'Miss Irene…today your best friend Christina is also present here. So, we have one witness…There should be no hesitation in bringing to the tongue what lingers deep in the heart!'

Having blurted this out, he paused all of a sudden. In the dimly lit surroundings, the half-burnt candle stood at the centre of the table. A good deal of it remained unburnt. Some hopes too had remained intact inside Liaqat. Riveting his gaze on the two young women, he suddenly bent forward to confess something…

'I…Liaqat Ali Khan entreat…Miss Irene to become my life partner. It will be my good luck and lifelong favour to me if you grant your assent to this request.'

Pindrop silence reigned over the table. Irene was of a progressive mindset as was her family. But this evening brought things to a head with the speed of a tempest for which the girl was not prepared. Christina's eyes were wide with amazement. Irene's heart palpitated at a pace she had never before experienced. It was thundering in her ears so resoundingly that she could barely raise her eyes to meet his. She felt caught in a whirling turmoil that raged within her. How would her progressive and liberal-minded family take this offer? It was a strange dilemma for her to resolve.

Irene could barely hear the clinks of the spoons and clashing metallic clamour of bowls and glasses, nor the burst of gay laughter and conversation which set the glamorous evening vibrating. In her mind streaked flashes of lightning of many volts.

'Please, take your time, Irene! I shall wait—though every minute of this waiting will be as endless as a century'.

Saying this, Liaqat scrutinised Irene's face and eyes in an attempt to read her emotions and reactions which rose and fell inscrutably. At that instant, Christina patted Irene's back to prod her to give some kind of reply.

'I need time'. Lowering her eyes, Irene could mutter only this much.

'Undoubtedly, I can understand your perplexity. I shall get in touch with you... fifteen days from now... That is the fourth Saturday of this month...here in this place, and at this hour of the evening, right?'

Eyes still lowered, Irene nodded gently. As they got up to leave, Irene stole a look at Liaqat and smiled faintly. At that instant, Liaqat knew that she was half-way to giving her consent.

Before departing, Irene turned slightly towards him

but words got stuck in her throat. Then Christina sang out the famous Urdu couplet to assist them both in saying what they wished to say:

'*Easy is not this love, just understand this*
A river of fire it is, we must drown in it to cross it'

In response, Liaqat smiled meaningfully at Christina, and then looking at Irene gave this suggestive reply:

'*It is not the fault of your eyes*
Yes, I was fated to be ruined.'

Irene laughed in a spontaneous surge of pleasure along with Christina and her face vied with the blushing rose flower spreading its joyous fragrance in the air.

To tell the truth, despite being Muslim, Liaqat's views about marriage were modern. He maintained good relations with his first wife as long as they were together, although this was a marriage contracted at a very tender stage of life, and broke down under its own contradictions. His parents had been unhappy with him for taking his wife Jehangira Begum without *purdah* to Shimla. But nobody could ever know the real problem that crept between them and what led them to decide to live separately. When they eventually got married, Liaqat had already spent four years living separately from his first wife. In such circumstances, Irene could not be blamed for disrupting this failed marriage of Liaqat Ali and his first wife.

On the Horns of a Dilemma

The ball was in Irene's court. She could not decide how she should move on this proposal. It posed a flabbergasting problem. Christina had pretty open and frank views. Despite the practical life views and approach of Christianity and her progressive convictions, Irene needed to muster the courage to go against the traditional thinking of her orthodox clan. She could not imagine the upper caste Brahmins of Almora ever endorsing a matrimonial alliance with a non-Brahmin person, leave alone agreeing to a marriage with someone coming from a different religion.

She found herself perplexed, at the crossroads, at a time when her attraction for this sober and liberal man was growing more and more every day. The more she thought about him, the more she felt drawn towards him. A strange magnetism indeed!

On the other hand, another road was open to her, a road that said 'No' to Liaqat's proposal but was safe and secure. At this crossroad, something seemed to compel her steps to a blind alley, a road that led to nothing but a dead end.

Many days passed in this confusion. No quick, easy means of conveyance were available in those days. Irene decided to visit her home in Almora next Saturday. Besides, there were holidays too. If the compulsion of going home had not been there, she would have certainly used this vacation to work on her PhD synopsis. Now she must talk to her mother and the rest of the family members. Her father was in Allahabad, but she did not think of confiding in him. Besides a certain 'No', she could expect to be subjected to many annoying lectures which she didn't have the stomach to digest! She had a bond with her mother but how emotionally sturdy or fragile this was, was yet to be put to test.

Irene sent a telegram to Liaqat regarding her trip home. In the meanwhile, another development took place. Before leaving for Almora, she received a letter from the person who was occupying all her thoughts.

With her heart hammering, she opened the envelope. Yes, it was Liaqat. He wrote:

Irene,
Perhaps you understand how every single moment of life is associated with different types of memories.

It is these moments that combine to create a distinct world for us. A world, when we reach it, where our pain and sorrows are set aside and we wish to immerse ourselves in our small pleasures. In that world only two individuals exist, one who loves and the other who gets loved, the receiver of it. All other matters then become redundant. Believe me, I have also dreamed of such a world; to fulfill it or just wipe it off is only in your hands. If you come and stand by me, this world will be beautiful. This life will be complete, otherwise, people just come and depart; neither do they know what has been their purpose in coming, nor does the world render them worthy of memory.

Promise me you will colour my dreams and provide fullness to my persona. Together we will create a world that all will remember; not merely remember but identify us with such a goal. You may attribute a different meaning to my proposal of marriage but the truth is that everybody is seeking some purpose in his life. I have found my goal—one, your company; two, the country's well-being. If you come with me, the path of the second goal will become easier; otherwise, I don't know in what wilderness this life will stray on its way.

One more thing. This proposal is forever. I shall continue to repeat my appeal. But it is also necessary to know that in declining it you will deny love to that person who not only cherishes the dream of doing something different for the country but also has a

dream of creating a new history.
Hope you be so good as to bear in mind the scheduled
date at Chelmsford Club.
Waiting for you,

– Liaqat

Earnestly in love, Liaqat revealed quite a different facet of his personality. Irene felt a great pressure, the weight of his expectations. Having read the letter, she collapsed in a corner of the sofa, unable to think. Her mind seemed to be in a frozen state. She read it again and again…but it appeared to her that though she was independent, she was hardly regarded as the sole master of her life. Like an ordinary Indian woman whose childhood is in the hands of her parents and elders, she could not decide in respect of marriage; it must be decided by them. Afterwards, a woman is under the care and control of her husband, and then her children exercise their authority over her.

Despite this awareness, Irene felt a peculiar thrill at the idea of accompanying Liaqat in the journey of life ahead. And the next moment a nameless terror shook her soul at the thought of this being denied! A question nagged her, 'Does this happen to everyone who falls in love?'

It is undeniable that she had also fallen in love but that love had to find the courage to knock down the restrictions hedging her in.

A while later, Christina came in the room and spotting the half-open letter and envelope, teased Irene with this Urdu couplet:

*'Whether you come or not, your message finished me
If you come, will my life be spared?'*

Irene could not help giggling at this new fad her friend showed these days of quoting Urdu couplets. But Christina was not done yet:

'I've begun to envy your luck, dear...Just think, if this is your condition right now what will happen after marriage! He will kiss the very ground you tread. Just see what poetic lines he has sent to his sweetheart!'

'That's enough! I can't understand matters of love by depending on Urdu couplets. This type of language suits you better.'

So saying, Irene got up to leave but Christina stopped her.

I'll tell you what Ghalib Saheb says:
*'Who knows what magic is that lovers seek in waiting!
Who poured it in their ears!'*

'Put love back in its place, Christina. Many other issues cannot be overlooked. To bind one's life with somebody is not a trivial matter; especially when you look at my conservative family. Do you believe they will ever break these shackles? I doubt. Then...'

Christina cut short her anxious outpourings to say:

'You have not understood even now, Irene. I'm not ready to accept this. What can be a better example of liberal thinking for a family which broke the shackles of religious narrow-mindedness to adopt another religion? When they can be influenced by the life-view and ideas of Jesus Christ, why can't they adopt those of Prophet Mohammad? The trick is to put forward your case logically.'

Theoretically, Christina was right. Irene didn't see it from this angle. But now she had a strong argument which put her on a firm footing.

'Let's see…'

Having said this, Irene hugged her. Christina had been able to show her a new path. It was Christina who brought it to her line of vision and gave her courage enough to walk upon it and adopt a new perspective.

A Fateful Journey

Christmas was around the corner. Her family usually began festive activities a week earlier. Irene's last class was the day after tomorrow, and then holidays!

Irene was having morning tea with Christina, when she asked her, 'Dear, could you get my ticket reserved up to Haldwani? The reservation counter is near your office.'

Stretching her limbs lazily, Christina yawned, 'God knows when my own ticket will be booked! The girl who stayed here before you also flew away like this. Eloped with an army officer! And here I am waiting… and waiting for someone to come along!'

Irene burst into laughter and went on laughing a bit hysterically. When she had composed herself, she said:

'Let's do one thing. We should switch roles. Now you

will meet Nawab Saheb instead of me…is it not a good idea to do role reversal…?'

'Wow! Whatever happens, you truly gladden my heart! It is important to keep up the light of hope, you know.'

Christina guffawed resoundingly.

Irene got her ticket confirmed. Lost in her dreams, she completed her journey to Haldwani by train. Her uncle's son Robert was present at the railway station to receive her. Whenever any lady of Irene's family had to be seen off or received, it was Robert's sole responsibility to do the honours. He had grown up before her eyes from an adolescent into a young man and to become the father of a son. People with his sense of responsibility were rare.

'Come, sister! Welcome home,' Robert said, hugging his younger sister.

'Oh, brother! You haven't changed…not even an inch! I can't figure out how you manage so much! I mean your business, your wife, son…and then caring for all, young or old. I know I can't even handle my classes coming one after the other. Start feeling giddy!'

They reached the bus stand by tonga-buggy from where they found a minibus that looked like it had come from a bygone era. These buses used to ply from Haldwani to Nainital and from Haldwani to Almora-Pithoragarh. Bus journeys in those days could hardly be called comfortable, nor were the roads easy to travel on. Old-fashioned, poorly maintained vehicles clattered all the way, speeding down battered roads. It was their good luck that they were going in cool weather, otherwise in summers, most of the journey was spent in wiping off perspiration. Even in those days, Haldwani was called the doorway to the enchanting mountain ranges of Kumaon valley. The same beauty and magic of Nature greets one today. This vernal Arcadia must have been a shade more beautiful then, for man's greed and rapacity had not begun to lay their dark shadows on it and swallow the blissful sights of green valleys and mountain sides.

Rolling meadows and lush forests luxuriated in Nature's sweet embrace and had become the identity of Haldwani. The place was named after a particular tree, the tree called *haldu*. The whole area thus came to be called 'Halduwan' or 'Haldwan'. Increase in population became the cause of destruction of the forest of Haldwani. In the rapidly expanding jungle of concrete and iron, this tree was desperately fighting a battle for survival. There was a time when it sprouted everywhere, in fact wherever its seeds fell the handsome trees would grow. Lack of moisture rapidly led to dwindling of the trees.

It is believed that in the fourteenth century, an Ahir ruler, Gyanchand, came here from the Delhi Sultanate. At that time, he had been granted an area Bhabhar-tari by the Sultan of Delhi as a gift. Later, Mughals tried to take it by force and launched many attacks, but its hilly terrain frustrated their attempts. A little before the first war of independence, in 1856 Sir Henry Ramsay took over as the Commissioner of Kumaon, but in 1857 Rohilkhand rebels succeeded in establishing their reign in the area for some time. This forced Sir Ramsay to impose martial law. However, by 1858, like other places in the country, this land was also flushed out of its fighters who had pledged to free the country from alien rule. In 1882 Sir Ramsay undertook to build a road between Nainital and Kathgodam and in 1883-84 a railway line was laid between Bareilly and Kathgodam. The first train became operational from Lucknow to Haldwani on 24 April 1884.

Four kilometres to the south of Haldwani, there is a region called Gora Padav where in the mid-nineteenth century there used to be a British camp. *Gora*, meaning white, had come to be metaphorically used for the British. Today we have a much better road between Haldwani and Almora, but if we visualise the facilities available in those days, we can appreciate what daring it needed to travel in those challenging times. Roads were pockmarked with potholes and broken patches. On one hand, fear of falling into one of them constantly followed the traveller; on the other, it was the fear of consigning your fate into the hands of a driver who knew no caution. Vehicles stopped at every small temple to seek the deity's blessing and if they did not stop, then grave reprimands were hurled for disrespecting gods. Drivers of buses and taxis could not think of going ahead without bowing their heads at such wayside shrines and paying donations. That practice still prevails unchanged.

Villagers must have enjoyed a good life but roads remained invariably wretched. A minor rockslide or mudslide, and the very life of travellers was thrown out of gear. Government help would arrive at snail's pace, hauling up heavy machines that had already become heavier and worn out, winding their way up the difficult hilly path to clear out the debris. And till they came, no one would know when the road would again be navigable. That confirmed the great faith in people's hearts in the existence of a God who looks after all our fates.

It was just a stroke of good luck that it was winter, and there was no possibility of rain with all its resultant problems. The weather was pleasant and the way to Irene's home was not so disconcertingly bumpy. So when Robert brought her home, it was thirty minutes past four.

In the shortened days of winter, the sun seemed to be in a hurry. The flushed pinkish glow had begun to fill the western sky and cast its magical hue on the skyline of the town of Almora. It was the capital of the Chand dynasty who ruled over Kumaon, but even before that, it was reputed to be the residence of the privileged Brahmins of the region. It is said that Raja Balo Kalyan Chand settled this town in 1563 and gave it the name of Alam Nagar. Earlier, Champawat used to be the capital of Chand dynasty. Realising the potential of this place, Kalyan Chand changed his capital from Champawat to Alam Nagar.

From 1790 onwards, the Gorkhas began to wage war on the Kumaon region. They attacked Kumaon and Garhwal and set up their rule here. Seeing this, Hastidal Shah of Nepal gathered his Gorkha soldiers and came down to defend Almora. On the other hand, a party of soldiers of the East India Company under Nicholas attacked the city on 25 April 1815 and effectively occupied it. On 27 April, Almora government's Gorkha officer Bam Shah surrendered, thus making it easy for the British East India Company to consolidate its position.

There is also a mythical tale about Almora. According to Manaskhand of Skanda Purana, a mountain is situated between the rivers Kaushika Koshi and Shalmali Suyal. This is the hill of Almora town. It is said that Lord Vishnu resides on top of this mountain. A section of episcopal scholars insist that Lord Vishnu's Kurmavatar or 'the tortoise incarnation' took place here. As per another mythical tale, a goddess of Almora named Kaushika Devi had slain two demons, Shumbh and Nishumbh at this very place.

Built in the last decade of the nineteenth century, Budden Memorial Church is famous for combining Roman and English architectural characteristics. The contribution of Irene's family was significant in its construction. Situated on the summit of the hill Malla Kasun, in the centre of town, this church offers a splendid view of Nature's rich diversity in every direction. Its construction was completed on 2 March 1897.

Popularly known as Almora's 'Bright End Corner', the place draws several loving couples to sit and watch the extraordinary beauty of the sunset and all the vernal grandeur bathed in the fading sunset glow. Its name was perhaps inspired by England's Brighton Beach.

Childish Pranks

Irene was born in this house on 13 February 1905 to Daniel and Annie, who already had two daughters. In all, there were eight children, the youngest being Henry (born in November 1921), still a toddler. When Irene passed her Grade 10 exam in first division with brilliant marks, there was a festive air at home. Her parents were so happy, they distributed sweets among neighbours.

Now Irene set her sights on Intermediate. It is only after passing this examination that she had a chance of competing for good jobs or could be counted as eligible for higher studies. Since her family had abandoned Hinduism and adopted Christianity, Irene could get a better education easily. Those were times when for girls and women the road to education in traditional society was either completely blocked or made quite difficult. Her present qualifications far exceeded what orthodox society was ready to sanction. For the Hindu community, a girl of Irene's age was now ready for marriage and she must marry. But her family's perception and priorities had by then undergone great change, having refused to be guided by Hindu precepts and doctrines. They did not make any difference between boys and girls as far as availing social opportunities was concerned. Both were seen as equal. And like many educated people, her parents too adhered to progressive ideas. There were many other Christian families where women could choose for themselves and get highly educated to stand equal to men, as compared to women belonging to other faiths.

Almora being a small place, despite Irene's good education, did not provide a conducive atmosphere to Christian women. Majority of the people appeared to be enamoured of their past and prided themselves in remaining stagnant. They regarded Christians as pariahs. The Christian way of life—their food, dress, behaviour and their faith—were a subject of contempt and ridicule. The Hindu word *mlechcha* (unclean) summed up the attitude of the upper caste chauvinists for non-Hindus, particularly Christian people.

One Gaura Pant, a relative of Daniel Pant's family and their next-door neighbour, adopted a similar attitude. Gaura, a prolific writer of her time, later wrote in one of her books while remembering them:

> There was the house of a Christian family, by the

name of Daniel Pant, close to our house who was related to us on my maternal side, but when they adopted Christianity, my conservative father built a sturdy high wall between the two houses so that any contact might not be made possible with them. We were not allowed even to look at them.

This Gaura Pant was the well-known Hindi novelist Shivani who is counted among the foremost literary figures of our times. Almora's lavish beauty and Nature's bounty appeared eager to find reflection in the writings of many sensitively gifted authors. Yet, indeed, Shivani did not live her own life in her characters nor did she in any way suggest the trials and traumas of Daniel Pant and Irene. It is another matter, however, that her family members, particularly her daughters, didn't hesitate to spin amusing gossip and anecdotes around this family.

Shivani often mentioned the aroma emanating from the house of Daniel Pant. They used to cook non-vegetarian dishes whose smell would upset Shivani's family, but nothing could be done about it. In her house would be cooked *daal,* gourd, *tori,* rice and *chapatis.*

Shivani's daughter Ira Pande notes in her memoirs:

At that time our grandfather used to live in Almora. There used to live a Christian family in our neighbourhood. Long past, the head of that family, Daniel Pant was related to us on our maternal side. But our traditionalist grandfather had strictly decreed that we should not even look in that direction and that ordinary-looking wall was the only cover against them. That's why the heady aroma of the non-vegetarian food arising from their kitchen, and wafting over the wall and into our house to overpower the simple smell of our *daal* and potato vegetable, and vanquishing it appeared to invade and completely enslave our nostrils. Windows and doors from the early hours of the morning were banged shut in a demonstrative show of our determination to prevent such an assault, accompanied by a shower of choicest abuses. But who could cover up the fine gaps and fissures? We used to meet their children clandestinely, partly because they were our blood relation, and partly because they led a more free and unrestricted life. The friendship tie was to us unbreakable. Henry in his sparkling shoes, striped socks, worsted half pants and stiff-as-stork's-wings collar of the shirt, and specially done hair, became our favourite. His sisters Olga and very lean Muriel would unhesitatingly come out in the flamboyant georgette sarees, nicely made up and unescorted to take walks. We simmered with envy as we saw them enjoy such unheard-of freedom.

Comparing his condition to theirs, Muku would stamp his feet in exasperation and say:

'What a life, by God! And here we are! Henry and Arthur eat eggs daily'.

'Without meat we cannot swallow a morsel, not

like you Hindus, always consuming green fodder!' Saying this, Henry would pour oil on the fire, and running his hand over his collar would leave whistling a tune to himself.

'Why do you forget, Henry, that your father and our maternal grandfather were once cousins? They must also be eating vegetarian dishes only'. Muku couldn't help saying. This had an instant effect on Henry.

'Now don't take me as a stranger. Let us think about what we can do for you. How will you face God if you don't eat meat! Now I will contrive something that will make you remember the smell of meat forever…the fragrance that will stick to your palate for a long, long time…But…'

Henry turned it into a big mystery. He fell silent now.

'Are you going to say something straight or just stand there creating more mystification?'

When Muku goaded Henry he spoke. He looked like a *pucca* trader! Henry leant against the pillar of the courtyard and said, 'If you accept the condition, I can say further…'

'Condition? What condition?'

Muku said and became quiet, but Henry was anxious to tell him; so he went on,

'You will have to pluck four apricots from your apricot tree and give them to me. Just four; no less, no more. But the condition is that you will have to smell all four in one go and just once, and before anyone sees you, you'll move forward. Are you ready?'

Was there time for Ira's brother to think? He saw Henry with his hands in his pockets blissfully reciting an English song.

'How mean is this, Henry?' muttered Muku to himself. But his greed took hold of his better senses. That aroma had been squeezing his heart. The smell was simply overpowering, mind-boggling. Then after a thoughtful moment, he said, 'Alright, then... conceded, four apricots for you! Done!'

Now the time was fixed and strategy decided. It was a challenge for both. Henry enjoyed a good deal of liberty, but for Muku it was a tough and dangerous mission, he had to work under strict restrictions. Crossing the iron-clad sanctions, Muku emerged in the gathering evening darkness. He had tightly tied four apricots, so tightly that it became a problem to untie the knot later on.

The time was fixed, but today that aroma had made up its mind to go straight into the nostrils which, mixing with the daily air, created such an intoxicating effect on the mind. God knows what special kind of smell it was! Till today its riddle remained unsolved. Anyway, the ladder that was chucked away neglectfully in a forgotten corner of the backyard was retrieved to the service. Putting it back into a useful form, the ladder was propped up in such a way that made it easy to go to the back of Henry's house. To land him there, the presence of Henry was needed. The Church clock struck ten. This is what was decided upon. So Muku climbed up. He had already become a restless soul, and on top of it, there came this maddening smell, the heavenly smell of meat curry!

Hearing sounds of Henry approaching on the other side, he felt a little easy. To put up a ladder against somebody's housetop was like breaking into it. Henry had brought his ladder used for whitewashing. It was also as dilapidated as Muku's ladder. But one more dramatic episode remained to be performed. One step was on the ladder and the other on the roof of the house when Henry whispered, 'Are you sure there are apricots?... no cheating, eh!' Muku felt a wave of anger, but one must be cool and use tactics and agility to come out of this nasty fix. He pointed a finger at the heavy knot, and the glow of victory spread over the persona of Henry. He signalled him to get down on the ladder.

With great caution, Muku began to step down. With a heart beating heavily he followed Henry. In the far corner, there was a pot boiling noisily on a disorderly pile of logs.

'Wow!' Muku exclaimed despite his resolution to keep quiet. Henry cautioned him angrily. When he got closer to the pot, the divine aroma hit him in that corner of the mind which never had such a blissful experience, nor had a chance of immersing in such a feeling. Folks often say that if such and such a work is not done, one may be deprived of both heaven and hell. And chances are that you may be sent back to the mortal world—to experience it. Similar was the condition of Muku. That celestial moment was just a few inches away now. The next moment Henry removed the lid from the pot, a whole world of enchantment floated up and sailed straight into his nose. It gave such an elevating feeling as can only be experienced to believe! Ah, yes. During this sequence of events, Henry demonstrated an amazing level of discipline. Even army men would envy him. Such fast action! Firstly, putting up the ladder, it was determined whether apricots had been brought or not; then getting down to take the charge of the fruits to inspect them closely… and then removing the lid off the pot in one snap action.

'Oh, brother! Please let me smell it a little more!' Muku whimpered, but Henry had adopted the attitude of a Brigadier. He said, 'That's enough! Don't be too greedy. This is all that was decided. Now get along…'

There was no room for negotiation or discussion. Muku sneaked off meekly. The aroma of meat curry smelt bland now and insipid because it gave the feeling of the sour grapes fiasco!

Shivani had other things to say about Henry, who was nearly her age. He was liked because he was different from anyone in her family and maintained an extravagant lifestyle. He would come in glittering leather shoes, a starched shirt and a smart tie. There were no restrictions on his two sisters Olga and Muriel's evening strolls either, while in Shivani's family even crossing the threshold was denied. Above all, when they used to wear lovely georgette sarees, a fire of jealousy consumed not only others but Shivani as well.

Shivani and other girls of the family were Brahmins of the reputed Kumaon and Almora family for whom even to think of such freedom was unpardonable. All they could do was dream of such an unhindered, unrestricted life. Bazars were far from their reach and girls could never think of visiting there, nor was it conceivable to decorate themselves in georgette sarees and ornaments. Everyone's eyes constantly followed the Pant family, which had lately turned Christian and closely noted their lifestyle. Special interest was shown in the liberty enjoyed by the girls as something extraordinary and out of this world. When they strolled through Lala Bazar, eyes would track them with curious interest wherever they went.

Hurdles in Love

When Annie heard the sound of approaching steps, she came down the stairway, taking ever faster and keener steps.

'Maa!'

It was Irene calling her mother, Annie. She put down her handbag and ran into the comforting embrace. After all, her mother was also her best friend. Whenever Irene encountered a problem, she'd come to her rescue like an angel. From birth to childhood, to the stage of adolescence when girls were confronted with baffling problems of physical changes that they felt disturbed about, it was her mom who explained things to her in such a convincing and reassuring manner that it instilled a sense of pride in Irene for being a woman.

'Oh, my child!'

Mother opened her arms and Irene became once again a tiny child. Caressing her back, she lovingly patted her as in the old days. When they disengaged, their eyes had become moist. It was as though they were meeting after ages.

Irene was the dearest child of her mother. This college lecturer had not only seen Delhi and Lucknow life but had also taught at Calcutta's Gokhale Memorial School after completing a teacher's training course from Calcutta's Diocesan College.

Stories about the Pant family's origin here do not portray them as hailing from some anonymous nook and corner of Kumaon or Garhwal mountains located in a village in the remote areas of this difficult terrain. Current lore has it that these people had their roots in Maharashtra. It is believed that four brothers from the Konkan region reached these mountains in the thirteenth century and made it their permanent home. Another theory lays down that about 25 generations back, in the year 1303 AD to be precise, Pandit Jaidev Pant left Himbara in Maharashtra to go on a pilgrimage to Badrinath. First, they settled like Joshis and Pandes, in the Kannauj area, but later trudged to the hills of Kumaon. Out of the four Konkani brothers who had gone to what is now Uttarakhand, three joined the profession of purohits (priests) and the fourth, Bhawdan Pant, became chief of the army. Three brothers remained vegetarian and his children too followed his ideal. But Bhawdan Pant and his children developed non-vegetarian habits.

The surname 'Pant' is still used for Pundits in Kumaon. It is believed that Pants were the principal religious teachers in Chhatrapati Shivaji's court. As per edicts, Shivaji's Prime Secretary Maheshwar Moropant was given 4,000 gold coins as annual salary and honoured with a seat in the front row of the court. When Allauddin Khilji attacked Ramchandra Dev, he compelled this ruler of Devgiri to accept and adopt Islamic religion. It was during this period that Pants, Joshis and Pandes scattered themselves in different directions of the United Provinces, Gujarat and South India to escape Khilji's brutalities.

The exhaustion Irene had been feeling after her day-long journey vanished when she met her mother. After she freshened up, they got busy talking about all sorts of things. However, Irene did not understand how to broach the one topic she had come all the way to discuss. Finally, she decided to put away all preliminaries and declare in clear terms, 'Ma, I'm ready to marry now.'

Her mother's joy knew no bounds. She joyfully took both of Irene's hands in hers.

'How come you are telling me today that which I always wanted to say? You are doing fine, dear. You do understand our feelings, no doubt. Now without loss of time I'll begin looking for a match for my sweet daughter... a matchless one, you just wait!'

She did not have any idea of the emotional turbulence her daughter had been passing through over the preceding days. How could she get a whiff of it when there had been no letters or any other kind of communication? Nor was it feasible for a daughter to explain everything in just one letter to her mother and settle the matter. There were inexplicable complications involved which Irene could fully appreciate. She could not tell how her parents and others would react but, in any case, the whole matter couldn't be postponed indefinitely. No harm, therefore, in letting an explosion occur. It is sometimes better to come straight to the point without a long preamble. She decided to lift the curtain without further ado.

'Ma! I've lightened your burden. The match approached me himself.'

'Is it so?' asked the mother. She could barely contain her pleasure. Choked with emotion, she hugged her again: no need to search, the match just came to her! She jumped to the conclusion that it must be a suitable match, her daughter being a sensible girl. How could such a proud girl proceed if she hadn't found the right person? That would spare her mother a lot of tension! Her joy and elation worried Irene. Slowly she was overtaken by fear.

'But Ma! Just listen. Won't you ask who it is that approached your daughter? What is his caste and whether he fits into your idea of an ideal husband for me? Or whether Dad would like him…or finally, such a situation may arise where I have to make my own decision?'

The close emotional chord between the mother and daughter tightened and strained painfully. It was close to snapping for some moments. Her mother was now alert and afraid. She looked deep into Irene's troubled eyes,

'What do you mean?'

'I mean to say that relationships are made in heaven. We are mere human beings. We were Hindus, now Christian, some are Muslim...others are Jews, Sikhs... God knows what else! But the source of everyone's origin is unknown, no? All must obey one sovereign God's authority. These faiths, castes, sub-castes, communities are not God's creation. These are the imagination of our thinking... the outcome of our narrow thoughts...'

Irene went on expressing her well-considered views on life; her surprised mother turned into a rapt listener. Ultimately, at one point, she interrupted, 'Look, Irene! There is no need to go into all this! I have always been an admirer of your plain speaking. Even now I like your frank, outspoken nature. My heart is not so fragile that anyone can smash it into pieces and walk away. But how do I know what's your point? You must be used to lecturing a lot in college. This lecture about caste, religion, community...what's the matter, honey? Tell me what is the issue.'

Annie was, after all, Irene's mother. She had gone through the agony of nursing her in the womb and giving birth. From birth till now, her mom had clutched her to her heart. Irene knew that. But when a child grows up, she must saunter out of the shade of the tree that sheltered it to seek the adult world. How could Irene be an exception? This was Nature's scheme, a preordained way the world moves and shapes our lives.

But how could Annie guess what Irene was trying

to say? She used to be a straightforward person, never mincing words or beating around the bush. What had come over her today? What conflicts were going on inside her? What is it that she wished to speak about but could not?

Irene paused for a while, then said, 'Listen, Mom! He is Liaqat; Liaqat Ali Khan, son of the Nawab of Karnal, educated at Oxford and active in national politics. At present, he is a Member of the United Provinces Legislative Assembly, elected from Muzaffarnagar constituency.'

'Please, Irene! Stop it! Do you realise what you're saying? Do you understand the meaning of marriage? It is a union of two hearts, two souls and two families and their cultures. Somebody comes along with a marriage proposal and you begin daydreaming! I've never heard of such a thing! Just pause a little to think cool-headedly why all these social systems have evolved—this caste system and all its attendant features and subsystems. There has to be a reasonable explanation. I'd say there is a scientific base to it.'

Her mother stopped for a little while to gather her thoughts. In this interval, Irene put in, 'Mom! I have been influenced by you and Papa. You two have been my role models. I have been proudly saying that the first attempt to oust these worn out, rotten systems and practices began in my family when you rejected the caste-ridden religious order and adopted Christianity. History repeats itself. The wheel has returned to the same point, having completed one round. Now the characters are a Christian and a Muslim. I see only this much of difference…'

There was stunned silence in the air. Both had made their points. Annie's displeasure surprised Irene and she wanted to change her opinion which didn't seem possible at the moment. Mom broke the silence, 'All this may be easy for you to say. But think about me. I'll be responsible for your actions, right or wrong. If it were possible, I'd have supported your choice. I'm not so mean…But…'

'But what, Ma?'

Irene looked into her mother's eyes and two drops forming in them were enough to threaten their relation. Wordlessly, Irene threw her arms around her mother. Then quietly she said, 'Oh, Mummy! I need your support. This marriage bond is created by us and in doing so we follow the standards made by us. Nothing can force us where love asserts itself. I didn't use reasoning when I fell in love nor was I guided by his position. But what I saw in him I found in no one else. In these conditions, if I say that I do not love him then that will be deceiving myself… And yet for your happiness, I'm ready to suppress my emotions. I shall forget there ever came a man in my life.'

Irene broke down between trembling words, her face sinking between her shoulders. Soon, she began sobbing uncontrollably.

'No, no, my child, do not cry. Since you were born, you must have seen your Mom standing by you in sorrow and joy. That is how a mother-daughter bond is forged. The umbilical cord is severed early but remains intact in another sense. In such a situation, I must honour your decision.

But matters are not as easy as they appear. Its impact will be felt in the next generation. I can't say how your Papa will react. He doesn't argue or discuss on the ground of logic or emotions, only declares his decision. Who knows, he may stand with you. Therefore, it'd be better to wait till he comes to give this matter its final shape.'

'But Ma, my holidays and the time of meeting Liaqat all are fixed. There can be no change in them.'

Irene dissented.

'Holidays can be extended. You can meet Liaqat afterwards, but instead of keeping the matter pending, it is better to talk it over with your father.'

The mother had made her stand clear. She did not approve of marriage with this man, but for the sake of her daughter's happiness, she was ready to bow down. This much she made clear. That the match would reach its conclusion was not easily possible. The opinion and consent of Irene's father were necessary. Irene decided to stay back. She sent a telegram to her college requesting an extension of her vacation by two days. But she had no idea how to reach Liaqat for postponement of their next meeting at Chelmsford Club. She had no means to do so.

It was another matter that fate had already decreed their union, and appointed a date for it. In bringing about this historic event, the contribution of Lucknow's multi-religious and multi-cultural mindset, the atmosphere of heterogeneous geniality in which she had been educated, the true sense of a high culture of tolerance and generosity and her burning urge to do social work was decisive. It also helped Irene significantly in her political journey. It not only groomed her into becoming a leader with an astute mind but inculcated an ability to assess the situation with flawless precision. It is said that the characteristic Lucknow social milieu of combined cultural streams made it easier for Irene to grow up into a polished Urdu-influenced personality. Her blossoming love with Liaqat and later on her transformation into Gul-e-Ra'ana were the exquisite results of her ability to adapt to the Urdu-speaking ethos.

Nawab Saheb

Liaqat was born in a Muslim Jat Nousherwani family on 1 October 1895. He was his father's second child. Liaqat was educated, a scholar who had unwavering faith in the principles of Islamic democracy. He had already made a frontline position for himself as a supporter of the Indian Constitution. Although he was born in Muzaffarnagar, a large part of which was a family *jagir*, he originally belonged to Karnal. It is the same Karnal where the immortal saga of Kunti and Karna was woven in memorable tales and then carried over for centuries from one generation to another.

British rule had conferred on his father Nawab Rustum Ali Khan the titles of Rukan-al-Daula, Shamsher Jung and Nawab Bahadur which placed him in high esteem in the eyes of the rulers. The Ali Khan family was among those few families whose *zamindari* (estate) stretched from Punjab to the United Provinces. Besides the villages close to Karnal, he possessed 300 villages as his own *jagir*.

After their death, his parents Rustum Ali Khan and Mehmooda Khan were buried in the precincts of their palace in Karnal. There was another imposing *haveli* (palace) of this family in Muzaffarnagar's Jansath hamlet, where once their rule prevailed.

It is rumoured that the British rulers were particularly friendly and considerate to the Nawab's family for the timely help they rendered during the 1857 uprising to British soldiers of the East India Company who had been desperately trapped. This helped to demoralise their opponents.

Liaqat's family had close contacts with the Indian Muslim thinker and scholar Sir Syed Ahmad Khan. His father cherished the ardent wish to have his son educated and brought up under the British system. In 1918, Liaqat completed his graduation in Political Science and Law. As soon as he completed his education, he was married to his niece, Jehangira Begum.

It is believed that the British government offered him a nominated Muslim post under the Indian Civil Service (ICS) which was the highest and the most coveted government post at that time. But he declined, for his sights were set on a political career. A few days after his *nikah* (marriage), he sailed for England. In 1922, he even began practising law but soon found that it was not to his taste. So he returned to India in the year 1923.

Having spent these years in England, Liaqat had come to understand that if India was to make any progress, the yoke of colonial rule must be thrown off. Keeping this in mind, Liaqat resolved to enter politics. From adolescence he had noted the unjust and discriminatory attitude the British used to adopt towards Indian Muslims and felt deeply hurt. He kept looking for an opportune time. Like all young people in those early days of political awakening in the country, young Liaqat was also charged with nationalistic feelings, but with time there occurred a marked change in his ideas. In 1923, top leaders of the Indian National Congress invited him to join the party, but he declined the offer. The same year, he aligned himself with Muhammad Ali Jinnah's Muslim League.

He was active during the League's Lahore Convention. In 1926, he contested the United Provinces Assembly elections as an independent candidate. Later, he founded an independent democratic party which he represented as a leader in the Assembly. He continued to remain a member of the Legislative Assembly until 1940, when he was elected to the Central Council. During these days he would regularly travel from his home in Karnal to Muzaffarnagar's Sujdu Kothi. While Karnal was his home, Muzaffarnagar was his workplace.

About his wife Jehangira Begum, history is silent; perhaps because by the time his political identity was taking definite shape, Irene had made an entry into his life, though unofficially.

Nawab Saheb was quite anxious to meet Irene. But she was neither in Delhi nor did she come to Chelmsford Club. Liaqat waited for hours, to no avail. Heavy-hearted with dismay and disappointment, he returned to Lucknow. From the next day, the Assembly was to commence its session, and it was of utmost importance for him to attend. But those meetings with Irene over a few days had caused such a stir in the hearts of both that each thought that they were made only for the other. He thought that some serious circumstances must have held her up and possibly Irene informed him in writing at his Lucknow address. But his dismay deepened when he found no missive there too. He waited for three to four days more, but when nothing about Irene could be known, he wrote another letter to her at her Delhi address.

Dear Irene,

I feel that there must have been some compulsion behind your inability to come. But that doesn't reduce my anxiety about why you didn't come. It is necessary to learn about you, so I'm writing. I have to go to Karnal-Muzaffarnagar the next Saturday, on 07. The same road via Delhi. I shall wait for you on the day at 7 in the evening. This will continue until I meet you, at least once.

I shall be thankful if you inform me about your well-being and decision.

– Liaqat

The year changed into January 1930 by the time this letter came into Irene's hand, but Liaqat Saheb's love story remained incomplete. Indeed, he could effectively narrate his own heart's travails, and any sensitive person or one who has felt the pangs of falling in love, could understand his predicament.

That Saturday, that is on 4 January 1930, once again Liaqat was found waiting for Irene in the lounge of Chelmsford Club. From 6.30 to 8.15, he drank many cups of coffee all alone. But not only did the coffee taste bland, such a long wait also seemed like endless anguish. Another interesting point is that some of the members of this exclusive Club either knew him quite well or were familiar with him. Unaware of their eyes constantly following him, he got busy drawing figures and lines, some doodles on the paper napkins. When he was tired of this, he began writing that day's happenings in his diary. The wall clock sounded eight o'clock, thus minimising any possibility of Irene's coming. On a blank sheet, he scribbled:

> *Irene,*
>
> *As promised, I waited for you when I should have been in Lucknow today, or in my constituency Muzaffarnagar. But certain decisions make it difficult to arrange our priorities despite our knowledge of their relative importance. Our meeting was arranged amidst this dilemma. But it must be clear to you by now that I'm not used to putting aside important jobs for long, and delaying the decision.*

Revolutionaries have split into two factions over the attack on the Governor-General and Viceroy of India, Lord Irwin; one, the Moderates and the other the Extremists. Mahatmaji is critical of this action on the part of the Moderates. I can't understand how to develop the middle path.

Here I sit in seemingly interminable wait in the middle of a vacuum that marks my time, surrounded by noise and tumult of the club; whereas, in New York's Grand Central Palace an Auto Show will start in a short while in which my favourite Cadillac's new model V-16 will be on display. In Lucknow political developments have picked pace. In any case, I can't bear to see any diminishing in the passion for going to any length to make sacrifices for the country. Even now I appeal to you…rather entreat you to come to me to make it easier for me to turn this urge into an unquenchable ardour. Irene, you must surely have heard the old tale of one added to one to make eleven. I'll be in Lucknow for the entire month. If you wish, you may send your letter to me there. I shall be waiting. I hope whatever news I receive will be for the good.

– Liaqat
Jan 4, 1930

Irene was fated not to come, so she didn't come. How could she come? A severe crisis had gripped her home, a crisis that showed no sign of abatement. It held the potential to destroy everything. Irene had not expected such stiff opposition from her father. It looked like the family was waving flags of extreme conservatism in a determined battle with modern ideas. She had known her family as bold and liberal fighters against the very orthodox, retrogressive mindset it had begun to show now.

Back Together

While for Liaqat, Irene had become a phantasmagoria, a difficult dream to possess, Irene had come to realise that it was not within her power to resist her parents who loved her a great deal and suffered so much for her sake. Marriage to a Muslim was not an easy prospect for Irene's parents to consider. She didn't want to hurt them. At the same time, there was a consolation: both understood fairly well that none was at fault. If anyone or anything could be blamed, it was the incomprehensibly unyielding conditions which perhaps, who knows, may become favourable in future.

Irene could not give a pointed response to Liaqat's letters though she very much wished to. The wheel of time moved on. People's discontent with the British rule went on mounting. The oppression unleashed against the natives became tougher.

Christina's absence from Delhi only added to Irene's difficulties. She had gone home later during the vacation, but she had more holidays than Irene. If she were available, much of Irene's burden would have been reduced by sharing it. But now she found herself in a strange trap, a tight corner where no one was available to console her.

Three letters had come and were piled one upon the other. Irene felt that she had not enough courage to open the letter that had just arrived that day. By a stroke of good luck, Christina was to arrive that day. Till then, Irene let the letter lie untouched on the centre table and went to prepare tea. She had a headache.

She had just taken out pots of tea leaves, sugar, cups and saucers and a tray when the doorbell rang twice. 'This must be Christy,' thought Irene.

She ran to the door. She was right.

'My dear, Irene! I missed you so much!'

With great joy, Christina clung to Irene, arms tightly thrown around her. She was herself eagerly waiting for her, and now that she had come, Irene wanted to cling to her.

'Same here, Christy...Life is a bore, no?'

Suddenly Christina moved away and peeping into her eyes said, 'Not at all, dear...at least not for you, Irene!'

There was confidence in what she said. In truth, she had no inkling of the developments that had taken place recently. But when she probed a little, Irene cracked and began to cry. Then she narrated the painful experience she went through in Almora.

Christina said, 'But even then, it wasn't prudent to have no contact with Liaqat Saheb. This cannot be a one-sided decision. There is at least no harm in intimating him about this unpleasant situation. Then it would be better to listen to your heart's promptings. I've heard it said that decisions taken in love have the force to undermine even the ties of birth. Irene, this is your father's resolve. That too prejudiced and one-sided!'

'That's the problem, Christy, that he is not willing to hear anything. Reasoning with him is of no use; I knew this before, but I didn't know why, I felt that he would heed the voice of my heart. He would try to understand the one who has made his way into my heart. I'm truly disappointed this didn't happen.'

Irene's throat choked with emotion and tears rolled down from her eyes. Christina pressed Irene to herself and said, 'Every problem has a solution. It is important and necessary to keep the ways open, but if you shut the windows and doors of your room how will the winds that carry love messages enter? I too live in your heart, Irene…if you respect me even a wee bit, you must write to Liaqat. Ask his pardon for not responding to his previous letters. You two may never be able to unite in that bond of which you and I have always dreamt, but still, a friendly relation can be maintained. Don't sink so low…You are only subjecting yourself to greater agony.'

Christina went on talking and Irene kept listening.

Suddenly all barriers to emotions crumbled and were swept away in the flood of sorrow and pain which rushed out of Irene's heart. She began to cry again without restraint, heart-rendingly. It appeared that anguish was oozing from every part of her body. While consoling her, Christina's eyes began to overflow. Her voice was shaking as she said, 'After all, why are we so made? The precepts which we formulate for our lives become an obstruction for us when the time to apply them to our children comes. But no matter, time will find an answer for us, for even those who do not want to listen to logic. Who knows, later they may come around to see your point and decide that their daughter's decision is right. Meanwhile, make it a point to write to Liaqat. Right now. In the meantime, I shall prepare a nice cup of coffee for you.'

Christina got up to go but Irene stopped her.

'No… No! You must be tired. You've just come. I shall get coffee for you.'

Holding down her emotions, Irene sat down to write Liaqat a letter as promised. Should she attempt not to tell all that had happened? But was it possible? He had been eagerly waiting for her letter. This is what she wrote.

Liaqat Saheb,

First of all, allow me to beg your pardon for not being able to keep my appointment with you at the Chelmsford Club and not able to respond to your letters, compelled as I have been under the circumstances. I suppose, had you been also pursued by such vexatious conditions you'd find yourself wracked by a sense of depressive helplessness as I've been these last few days.

At the moment I've not much to communicate with you. But this much is sure that I'm still your ardent admirer and wish that we remain in touch with one another.

Regards,
– Irene.

What did this letter convey? Perhaps nothing much. But for Liaqat these few lines contained a world of meaning. It took no time for him to understand the harsh reality hidden behind them. He sensed that for now, Irene couldn't come into his life. But he could intuit that it was also not impossible. He had seen more of this world than Irene had done in the real sense. He knew that hopes had not died and that he must keep his patience.

And then Saturday arrived like the scented breeze of a new morn. Irene was once again there at Chelmsford Club. After almost a month and a half, the corner of the dining lounge and the dining table where they used to sit often had once again come alive. Yet there hung a strange calm between them. Liaqat didn't want to mention anything that would prevent her being at ease. He started the conversation:

'For me also, Irene, hills hold a strong attraction. Lucky you are to have been born in Almora amid such heavenly surroundings. Though I have not ever gone there, I can feel the thrill of being in the midst of hills of other places. Their very images transport me to another world. The green turf-covered acres, the heady, perfumed breezes that brook no barriers, the fountain of melodious notes thrown by the birds, trees and plants weighed down by flowers and fruits of diverse kinds, panoramic haze-shrouded ranges of mountains, the joy of walking over uneven paths, the exotic dwelling places made of local bamboos and wood—these lead you into the unexplored sources of pleasure and bliss that are your own. Far from the madding crowd's ignoble strife!'

This honest portrayal of the mountainous countryside brought a new spark in her eyes. What she wished to tell anyone about these beauteous regions couldn't have been better expressed. She felt grateful to her dearest companion for letting words create such a magical spell. She could say only this much, 'It is this that makes me lose control over my emotions and I let myself flow in the current of your voice…that's one reason I like you, you talk as I would have talked. I feel you are the measure of my personality.'

Liaqat was pleased. He said with gusto, 'Irene, after meeting you I tried to find out more about Almora. Though I have not seen it personally, the very thought of Almora reposing on the peak of a hill, opening out to an idyllic world of enchanting hills and forests and the limitless expanse of blue sky lifts one to a different level. Down, far down below, there must be a flowing Koshi river on one side and the other Suyal….'

Cutting him short Irene said, 'Truly said. It's like sitting in God's land. Such overpowering beauty! Every season there is fun and lure. If we compare it with the life that we lead in the plains, we realise how artificial our lives have become…to the farthest extent of our sensitivity and emotions. How good that those hill-folks are so natural!'

Liaqat kept his gaze glued to the beaming face of Irene, who was bubbling over with the joy of visiting the mountains and valleys of her birthplace like a child and listened to her engrossed descriptions. He loved the vivid force of her words. He shared with her the theory of the origin of the Pant clan, according to which in the mid-tenth century the famous Vedic scholar Jaidev Pant of Bharadwaj *gotra* had undertaken a pilgrimage from Konkan with his family. The wife of his brother, Dinkar Rao, who was a Parashar Brahmin, was accompanying them. The ruler of Almora at that time had granted them the *jagir* of Rikhadi and Uprada villages with the condition that they would stay there and assist the administration while training the next generation in Vedic knowledge. Apparently, to the Pant family the attractions of the place were strong enough. Thus they adopted Almora. These people of Bhardwaj *gotra* tenaciously followed the Vaishnav tradition and were strict vegetarians. Though scholars are divided in their opinion whether Jaidev had been a Chitpavan or a Saraswat Brahmin, inexplicably, later on, they dropped their *gotra* name and preferred being known as the ruler's court people and Pant.

Liaqat, having been educated in England, was a liberal Muslim. He had also made a study of theological subjects which carried his academic interest deep into the nature, character and origin of diverse religions, faiths, civilisations, cultures and histories. It pleased him to see that whichever topic interested Irene, she attained complete mastery over it—never were any gaps or blank spaces left. She also possessed a brave disposition to enter into debate with a mature clarity and force of conviction. That's one reason why Liaqat got so bowled over by Irene's energetic personality. He saw the inner gifts and sources of her unique merits that enriched her character. Wasn't it why he so ardently wished to spend the rest of his life with her as her husband?

'Did they live in Almora from the beginning?' Liaqat looked at her and asked.

'No. In the beginning, they settled in two separate villages and afterwards spread out to other places. But the majority of Pants went with their Raja or ruler to settle in the year around 1565, at a place which today is known as New Almora city. Even today, the family deities of those first Pants are preserved in those villages. Prominent among these villages are Uprada, Jajyut, Chitai, Kalsel, Barset, Khantoli, Mana and Khoont. Of these Pant families, the most aggressive and generous happened to be Sharam Pant. When Upreti Brahmins were expelled on the charge of rebellious temperament, it was Sharam Pant who challenged the decision and had to face expulsion from the royal court as a consequence.

This showed their stubborn nature which earned them the name of Hathwal Pant (*hath* being the Hindi word for adamancy or stubbornness). A few committed Pants called them Besharam (shameless) Pant.'

'Fantastic! What a unique treasure of information, Irene!' said Liaqat.

'No one can tell what the future will bring; one must spend an honourable life and live it meaningfully. It is one's duty to have a complete hold over one's life. Every moment is precious. And under the conditions prevailing in the country, who can say how things will turn out? It is of utmost importance for us to show our commitment and make whatever sacrifice we can. Only in that case does the welfare of the land make sense. As for our relationship, I can only say this that we must be lifelong friends, understand one another and if possible spend our lives together. The rest is in God's hands!'

Irene sat with downcast eyes. Whatever she could muster the courage to tell Liaqat, she had narrated. She had also made it clear that despite being converted to Christianity, her family continued to cling to the roots of their Brahmanical orthodoxy and felt peculiarly devoted to it. It was not so easy to get rid of it or destroy it. In small places, these roots and allegiances are more rigid, so much so that even when the slightest effort is made to deviate into progressive and liberal paths, fetters fall around the feet of bold persons. It is their nature to hold tenaciously to the ground. They do not understand that when new seedlings sprout or the chicks of a bird learn to fly, they seek the open air and limitless sky. Confining these new forms of life would be their death.

This was precisely Irene's condition. Her Mom was, no doubt, by her side, a little subdued, but there was left in her no courage to once again break the shackles that had clamped them to these irrational conservative doctrines. In these circumstances, it was best to leave the matter to Time. But was it possible?

Like her, Liaqat also felt the extreme pain of living under a rule that, despite the populace's views, was thrust on Indians and also felt the bitter pangs of not having her beside him in his struggle. This urgency for her company had the potential to change history.

Nevertheless, this meeting between them was not without importance. These two not only demonstrated their abiding affection for one another but also promised to keep in touch. Liaqat came to drop her at the house of her landlord in Old Delhi's Sitaram Bazar where she lived with Christina as a paying guest. The house owner was Mallik Malkhan Chand of Karnal. Even today his family lives in Karnal. He chose to live in Delhi with his wife and two sons as he had his business there. But he kept visiting Karnal periodically. As it chanced, he had also reached home when Liaqat came to see Irene off. Malkhan Chand's pleasure at seeing him knew no bounds. He never imagined that his Nawab would appear at his home in such unusual circumstances. Surprised at seeing him at his door, he said, 'Sir, you? Please come. You haven't recognised me, perhaps. We are your lay subjects, your highness.'

With profuse entreaties, Malkhan took Liaqat inside the house which was very large and built in the old style. His family was engaged in wholesale trade, buying and selling raw spices not just in Karnal but in all the shops of the villages located in the surrounding areas. They depended on spices procured by him.

Liaqat accepted Malkhan's hospitality with eagerness since he was keen to get acquainted with the conditions in which Irene lived. Christina too appeared and was pleased to have a distinguished guest. After tea, Liaqat took leave of them and promised to keep in close touch with Irene. In any case, the names given by formal relations do not matter where the heart creates unbreakable ties, Liaqat might have thought.

Together Forever

When she began her education, Irene used to be the only girl student in her class at Lucknow University. She evinced a keen interest in studies. That explains why she topped the merit list of Master's in Economics and Sociology. Her dissertation topic was 'Women Labour in the Agricultural Sector in United Provinces'. In it, she dealt with an overview of the prevalent conditions and besides that also offered an assessment of the role of the new generation of rural women. The dissertation received much acclaim from the faculty and appreciation from her examiners and was adjudged the best thesis of the year.

The love between Liaqat Ali and Irene Pant bloomed as if it was rooted in the ground of unflinching loyalty and willingness to make sacrifices in circumstances which made its path difficult and uncertain. With great devotion, both pooled their time and thoughts to grapple with the social and political issues of society. All the while, it was clear that their journey along this road was besieged with struggles and difficulties. It appeared that the intensity of passion for the social world was also equally high. Somehow their love for one another imperceptibly mingled with this passion and grew on its emotional strength to make them yearn for each other. They had no idea how their goal would be achieved, nor whether the road they travelled would lead to that goal. Yet there was this love for one another, deep, unshakeable and ever-growing.

Irene had earlier gone to Calcutta for a Teacher's Training course. She loved living in Calcutta—she thought the city and its culture suited her temperament. There she met Kay Miles, whose friendship offered her a much-needed assurance and relief. By the time Irene finished her course with top marks, she was also getting involved in Calcutta's social and cultural life. She was deeply influenced by Jamini Roy's paintings, which made a considerable impact on her. They gave her a clearer awareness of the Bengal renaissance and the peasants' lives. She was able to meet Kay Miles only on weekends.

Having topped the course, it was easy for Irene to get job offers from local schools. She began teaching at the Gokhale Memorial School and continued in employment for about six months. This school was run by the former

Brahmo Samaj worker and educationist Sarla Roy. It was a girls school dedicated to Gopal Krishna Gokhale, who had pioneered the nationwide movement for women's education. He firmly believed in scientific and technical education in providing a strong base for a powerful, self-reliant India. Self-government and strength of character depend upon an individual's abilities. But building a new society is possible only when women are also allowed to participate in equal measure.

However, there was one serious problem. The humid weather of Calcutta was affecting Irene's health. She started feeling unwell most of the time. It was in these circumstances that she received a letter from her sister Shanti bearing a ray of hope. Shanti and her barrister husband had a permanent home in Patna but for some time the couple had been camping in Meerut as her husband was a counsel in the Meerut Conspiracy Case. Shanti came to know that a post of lecturer of Economics had fallen vacant in Delhi's Indraprastha College. She immediately wrote to Irene about it. It was a golden opportunity for her in two senses: she would be teaching in Delhi's most prestigious college, and it would make it easier for her to meet Liaqat Ali. Her selection in that college makes an interesting story.

She posted an application based on a newspaper clipping of the advertisement. She met all the criteria. The college had started post-graduation courses that very year. Other competitors stood a good chance, but after some discussion among the selection committee members, Irene was found suitable for the post. Irene was happy; her heart's desire was going to be fulfilled. Leonara G'meiner, an Australian lady, was the Principal of the college at that time. Indraprastha College was the first institute of higher education for women in Delhi, established by the well-known social activist Lala Jugal Kishore at the call of Annie Besant. But it was considered a tough matter to get selected as interviews were rigorous. It was natural for Irene to feel nervous and somewhat diffident.

A social worker, Leonara dreamt of educating Indian girls. What she started as a school in 1905 became a college running graduate courses by 1922. It was good luck for Irene that by 1930, post-graduation courses were about to commence. Madame Leonara was known as an educationist free from any sort of bias; she wished to stay in India and boost the educational movement for women. But in those days, challenges were numerous. In the interview, Irene left a deep impression on her; however, there was pressure for another candidate Mrs Sen Gupta. Finally, Irene was selected. Irene did not want any favour or bias in the process; she knew her worth as surpassing all others. After that came the question of salary. Irene needed time to think. She wanted to be capable enough to meet the demands of her lifestyle and her status in a city like Delhi. The offered amount was not in any sense inadequate but she decided to discuss the matter with her family.

On 18 September 1930, she wrote a letter from her home in Almora to the Principal of Indraprastha College.

> *Dear Madam,*
> *I hereby accept your offer of the salary of Rs 200/- per mensem. I shall be grateful if you take an early decision on this matter.*
> *I shall leave Almora on 27 September. My new address will be as follows:*
>
>
>
> *Care of Mr J.N. Mukan*
> *Nazar Bagh,*
> *Lucknow.*
> *Yours Sincerely,*
> *Sd/- Miss I.M. Pant*
>
>

Till today, the college has preserved the correspondence between Irene and the college.

This was a time when Rs 200 a month was considered a princely sum, equivalent of today's Rs 2 lakh per year. To teach in a college that was rated the best women's college of the national capital provided her great pleasure. Out of her monthly pay, only Rs 25 was paid for house rent.

The Principal first thought of putting Irene in a women's hostel at the Young Women's Christian Association. But the waiting list there was fairly long. Therefore, she agreed to find a room for her at the Girls' Friendly Society Hostel. Later on, she found for herself an independent accommodation with one of her friends, who shared with her the rent and other expenses. Those days Hindu women were not willing to work with men, and even if some girls were prepared to do so, such pressure was put by the family that they preferred not to work at all. This resulted in most of the employment chances being grabbed by Anglo-Indian women. If she had stayed there after obtaining a degree from the Teachers' Training College and had been absorbed there, she would not have met the Nawab nor would those meetings have turned into a love affair.

In the meantime, another incident occurred. Liaqat Ali Khan was invited to deliver a speech at Indraprastha College. This pleased both—Liaqat was being conferred an honour by the college and Irene was feeling proud about it. This was truly a special day. He arrived in the auditorium at the appointed time and was escorted to the podium by the Principal. After talking a little about himself, Liaqat began to refer to those problems which were responsible for the deterioration of general conditions in the country.

> The country needs such colleges as Indraprastha College has proved to be. I witnessed this dream assuming concrete shape right before my eyes in Lucknow. The same hands that built this institute also created there the Isabella Thoburn College. Of course, the organisations are different, and the names may also be different. But the point is of principle. We have now come to the full realisation, albeit late, that in all corners of the world women's education is as necessary as that of men.
> Not only this, I would say that more efforts should be made to impart education and training to women in many areas than men because men

are involved in the problems of employment, but women have to fight on every front and find answers to the home front as well as out-of-home questions. Better management and patience are expected of them. It is said that if there is one educated woman in the family, the whole family is educated. But if only the man is educated and the woman remains illiterate, nothing short of a miracle can improve the children's lot.

The level of education that we expect in the present circumstances appears to be a mirage. But no effort goes waste. One and one make eleven, I believe. Mobilisation of public opinion is important, political will comes later. It is necessary to have a social and educational awakening. If Indraprastha College decides to lead the nation in this matter India's future is bound to remain in secure hands. This I say in full confidence!

Mention was also made by Liaqat of the efforts he had been making in the United Provinces, but the focus of his address was mainly on women empowerment through education, although the subject he was called upon to talk on was 'Law and Justice'. His speech concluded to resounding applause as the auditorium reverberated with ovation. Irene, who was sitting in the front row, felt proud and kept smiling.

It was, perhaps on this day that Irene decided to put an end to all her dilemmas. Her heart was finally resolved to accept Nawab Liaqat Ali Khan's proposal and accept him as her life partner. She had begun to regard the old traditions, beliefs and religious restrictions as meaningless. Of their own volition, her feet turned in the direction of his love. By then Irene had come to know him thoroughly through diverse means and in full measure. Besides religion and politics, his opinions about women accorded with those of Irene, which is the reason why they struck such a harmonious chord between them.

Liaqat's first wife was his close relative. They happened to be the same age and had played together in childhood. Initially, they had quite a happy married life, but later on, no one knows how, differences arose between them. Soon these differences began to cast shadows over their feelings for one another, compelling them over time to live separately. This occurred in 1928. They had understood that their paths could never converge and must remain separate. He felt ensnared by his love for his son Vilayat, born of Jehangira Begum.

Irene's enthusiastic Principal Leonara, unmindful of Irene's relationship with Liaqat, was extremely happy to get a very efficient and intelligent lecturer in her. Once, however, she had a strong reason for complaint against Irene which concerned not with the academic performance but with the administration. Irene put before her a demand for a pay increase. The Principal wrote about it to the Chairman of the management body, Jugal Kishore, who did not refer to her teaching methods or other deficiencies, if any, but underscored that she took only three periods per day, yet she felt that her salary was not adequate, perhaps because she is in the habit of wearing expensive dresses and jewellery and could not meet such needs in this amount. What is regrettable is that after Irene left the college, the Principal wrote to the Chairman another letter in which she said, 'Despite all her weaknesses I should have continued her in employment and concentrated on her service. She was not all that bad.'

As long as she was there, Irene earned the goodwill, affection and respect of all. She spent one-and-a-half years in Indraprastha College during which she was able to create a long list of admirers. Her decision to leave caused great dismay amongst her students, the faculty and the non-teaching employees. But she couldn't stay there. When Irene put in her resignation, her friend Christina had also left a little before to take up a good job in Bombay.

The lonely condition of her life rendered it difficult for her to stay in Delhi. Nawab Saheb remarked, 'Oh no! It'd be better for you to stay in Delhi. You can't come out once you go to Almora. In my opinion, this is not proper, at least for the time being…'

'But there has to be a reason for staying in Delhi. How much savings do I have…? Without a proper job, I can neither meet my expenses of day-to-day living nor live comfortably. It is necessary to be practical.'

Liaqat thought differently. He made a suggestion which he had not put forward till then because there had arisen no need to do so. He told her: 'I've two offers. A nice, decent place for your comfortable stay, and a preoccupation to make use of your leisure time: work that would suit your disposition, brain, liking and standard. Don't refuse, please!'

Irene looked at him closely. He was serious. There was nothing in his eyes but love and honesty. After a little pause, she enquired, 'What sort of job is it? And what is that place where I'm supposed to live?'

'Any institute with which you associate will feel honoured to have you. I run a trust through which I try to bring the society's have-nots, helpless and the wretched of the land into mainstream life. My trust seeks to identify village women engaged in some employment and aims to raise their life by giving them proper training. Since you have made a study of such women, I think there would be no one more eligible for the job than you.'

She interrupted Liaqat, 'That's all fine, Sir! What about my accommodation?'

'Exactly! Do you know the Maidens Hotel? A suite in it will be your temporary living quarter and the working address of my trust. Necessary staff will be provided plus food and other requirements. Every need of yours will be taken care of.'

For a while Irene was quiet then she said, 'Certainly the idea is excellent and suits my taste, but I'm afraid it will become a burden on you…Or may start incurring all unnecessary expenditure which may raise other ideas in your mind…'

'Oh, no! Nothing of the sort. This trust is very close to my heart. But despite my efforts, I could not quite get it off to a working level. You know my unorganised way of life…one job finished, another comes along, that completed, the next leaps forth…an endless procession which will keep hounding me till I die!'

Liaqat had become emotional; Irene stepped in to lighten the air. It was after a long time that they were meeting in Wenger's. This café and Chelmsford Club had treasured many a tale of their meetings. Liaqat's offer had made them both complementary to one another.

'Liaqat Saheb, trust me, I consider it my duty to complete your unfinished projects. I've known you for some time and gauged your depths. If a few more people of your thinking come along, no one can stop the country from developing into a strong, independent and prosperous society. I shall consider it my privilege to be associated with any task you give me and make all efforts to fulfil it. You can rely on me!'

This was accomplished in one coffee session. Maidens Hotel was the first starred hotel in British Delhi which had then been newly built. It was set up by two Maidens brothers who completed its construction in 1903. This was the time when the British might in India was at its height when steamers and steam railways used to be the only means of transportation and conveyance. That must surely have been an exciting time! The hotel was reserved for British officers, army officials, big landholders and a few select entrants with acceptably high social standards.

It represented the finest specimens of British colonial architecture and is even today preserved as an exclusive legacy. For Irene, it was like a fantasy-filled dream to live there and most lovingly put colours in Liaqat's dreams—a fabulous journey. For herself, it stood as a gateway to a deeply personal exploration of a remarkable experience—an experience that enriched every single moment of hers in a wide spectrum of political and cultural engagements.

Every corner of this hotel treasured some unique fable connected with the opulent living style of the royal families or their valour and the minor *jagirdars*' family festivities or Delhi Durbar. In those days there used to be just one address for any memorable celebration: Maidens Hotel.

The time which Irene spent here remained etched in her memory forever as the most cherished period of her life, when she could live and utilise her time as she wished, without anyone telling her what she should do! Amid the early morning chorus of peacock calls and the air bristling with the full-throated melody of all kinds of birds, Irene's soul blossomed like a pure lotus, smiling and wondering at the turn of events in her life.

The hotel stands today in all its past splendour, undiminished by time's passage, in the ridge area of Delhi. It is now a heritage hotel and is the property of the Oberoi Group of Hotels. It still exudes the same warmth of hospitality, located at 7, Sham Nath Marg, Civil Lines, Delhi.

During the period of her stay in this hotel, Irene moved further close to Liaqat's heart. Most of the time he kept commuting between Lucknow, Karnal and Muzaffarnagar, but Delhi remained tucked away in some corner of his heart, mainly because it was the capital of the country and more importantly because it was also the seat of the queen of his heart.

Then one day it came to be known that *nikah* had been performed between Irene and Liaqat Ali Khan and they were married. All rituals of the wedding were solemnised in Maidens Hotel itself. There was perhaps no one from her family to attend the celebration, but some of her close friends and associates turned up with their joyous and sparkling presence. From Liaqat's side, there was a strong presence of his big family and friends.

As per Muslim law, Liaqat was permitted to marry a second time without divorcing his first wife Jehangira Begum. He took care to see that she didn't suffer financially. Income which came from his land holdings and property in Karnal went to his first wife and their son. For his own expenses, he drew only Rs 500.

It was not known whether he divorced his first wife, but there is nothing to suggest that this second marriage created any differences or disturbance in the family or unpleasantness in any one of his relationships. This became clear from the huge attendance of his relatives. The date of their wedding was 16 April 1933. Plenty of water had flown under the bridge by this time. In truth, this cannot be described as a case of love at first sight. There were sufficient meetings and conversations between them in which all topics and facets of public life such as Hindu-Muslim issue, women's problems, domestic and foreign affairs came up. Each knew the other's views perfectly. The marriage had by then become a foregone conclusion and only the solemnisation of relations remained. Irene accepted Islam to facilitate an easy and prompt wedding. She was rechristened as Gul-e-Ra'ana and later came to be called by an abridged form of it, Ra'ana. People preferred to call her Ra'ana Liaqat Ali or Begum Ra'ana.

Delhi's Jama Masjid is regarded as the most important centre of religious faith and its Imam is held in great esteem. Liaqat-Irene's *nikah* was performed by the then Imam of Jama Masjid. Liaqat's elder brother Nawab Sajjad Ali Khan was present on the occasion as the senior-most member of the family and bestowed the newly married couple with special blessings for a happy life. He held a big function on the occasion for the elite of the capital and his district.

It can be said that by marrying Irene, Liaqat played a political masterstroke. He acquired a wonderful life partner, a political advisor, a fine friend, a historian, economist and a champion of women's causes. He was enchanted by every part of Irene's personality. They proved an ideal couple: he lent such complete support to her that she could not think of herself as a complete woman without him nor could he for that matter think of himself as a complete man without her.

From Lucknow to Delhi

Lucknow of 1930-31 was quite different from today's Awadh, but it was as much known then for its exquisite, refined etiquettes and multi-cultural society, Dussehri mango orchards and the *chikan* embroidery work as it is now. The cultivated tastes of its Shia Nawabs provided all-out protection and patronage to its celebrated codes of behaviour, beautiful gardens, music and savoury dishes. Lucknow has always been known as the City of Nawabs and came to be fondly called Shiraz-e-Hind and Golden City.

Going back into ancient history, it is believed that what came to be called Lucknow was once part of the Kosal empire. Lord Ram inherited it and handed it over to his brother Lakshman, hence it came to be called

Lakshmanawali, Lakshmanpur or Lakhanpur, which over a period of time mutated into Lucknow. Subsequently, the old Hindu Rajas gave way to Muslim rule. The Sheikhs came in the year 1160 along with Mahmud Ghazni's nephew Saiyyad Salar leading an invading army. The first thing he accomplished was the construction of a sturdy fortress at a place where Machchi Bhawan was located. Its famous strength was attributed to a person named Likna Ahir. Hence, the fort came to be called Likna Qila.

In 1540, Mughal emperor Humayun marched to Jaunpur where he was soundly defeated by Governor Sher Shah. Humayun crossed Sultanpur, Lucknow, Pilibhit and Kashmir to return to his home. He made a halt at Lucknow for four hours, during which time his badly beaten, despairing, frustrated and hopeless army saw the inherent cheerfulness of the city and felt overwhelmed by it. The Sheikhs of the city not only procured for him 10,000 coins at a short notice but fifty of the finest horses as a token of their hospitality. This was sufficient to reveal the generous, opulent culture of the region.

Another legend goes that the city was named after the main architect of Likna Qila, Maharaja Lakhan Rajput. If we put aside these semi-mythical and unconfirmed legends, it is a historical fact that Lucknow as a city was established by Asaf-ud-Daula in 1775. Succeeding rulers of Awadh no doubt enriched it in various ways and raised its artistic and cultural levels in a manner that it became one of the most beautiful cities. But it cannot be denied that the succeeding line of Nawabs proved to be so utterly debauched and idle that Lord Dalhousie hardly faced any resistance in capturing Awadh and assimilated it into the empire of East India Company. All that these Nawabs were good for was guzzling quantities of liquor all day and night, excess of sensual pleasures, unending spells of idleness and inventing new kinds of physically titillating pleasures, unmindful of the grave political crisis that was building up and was soon to wipe them out.

From Asaf-ud-Daula to Wajid Ali Shah, no one paid attention to the problems of the people who depended on the rulers for their survival. The Nawabs were preoccupied most of the time with women coming in and going out of the durbar; they gathered around them all conceivable means of a luxurious living that set no limit to the sensual pleasure they constantly hankered after. For this, they were entirely dependent upon their servants and petty officers. The state officers, called *aamil*, used to have the responsibility of collecting revenue. These officers were assisted in their jobs by an 80,000 strong army always in readiness.

Half of this revenue went for the upkeep of the Nawabs. *Aamils* and other officers normally displayed an open, unabashed tendency to unscrupulous behaviour and lack of character, often resorting to bribing court authorities in various ways to retain their posts. The procedure of tax collection was invariably accompanied by blatant harassment and cruelty perpetrated on the wretched masses. The poor people not only had to pay taxes far beyond their capacity but undergo humiliation and physical cruelty at the hands of the collectors. Rich *zamindars* who lived in luxury and comfort in their huge palaces and forts enjoyed complete exemption from these taxes.

This naturally led to the depletion of revenue and gave rise to deep dissatisfaction among the masses against the rulers. As a natural consequence, crime increased appallingly and threatened to disrupt the common man's life. Theft, banditry, loot, plunder, murder and violent attacks in public places became common occurrences. There was no let-up in these incidents; neither was property safe nor life. Conditions appeared ripe for a popular uprising against such decadent and immoral ruling clique.

In 1849, the Governor-General Lord Dalhousie directed the Resident of Lucknow, Major-General Sir William Henry Sleeman to undertake an extensive tour of entire Awadh and prepare a detailed report on the ground realities and present to him. The report which Sleeman put before him was a voluminous document containing astonishing figures of crime on the rise, exploitation and endless woes that marked the life of common people, all of which he himself had witnessed. Large arable chunks of land were fast getting transformed into barren wastelands, overgrown with untamed jungles and endless stretches of bramble and brushwood. Every highway and public place was dotted with such criminals who would lure travellers and snatch their belongings by deceit. Slightest resistance would mean instant murder executed with professional efficiency. To confirm the account present in it, the Governor-General once again asked the new Resident, Col. Outram to make an investigative tour. His report didn't differ much from the previous one.

The British government felt assured that the situation had gone completely out of the hands of the Awadh rulers and, therefore, as a move towards improving it, proposed to draw up a pact according to which the military and general administration of Awadh would be permanently taken over by the British. It was agreed that the Nawab's family would continue to get the honours which they had been enjoying for a long time. Another point in this agreement related to the male heirs of the reigning Nawab, who could retain regular courtly honours. They would exercise their sovereignty over the areas known as Bibiyapur and Dilkusha Palace. For their expenses, they would receive Rs 12 lakh per annum and for the maintenance of security guards an additional Rs 3 lakh. Lucknow was six miles from east to west and in width four miles. Now the Nawabs' time of reckless living was over and they needed to exercise extreme caution. After three days of consultation, Nawab Wajid Ali Shah declined to sign the agreement. This provided to the British the opportunity they were looking for. Following a formal official proclamation, the state of Awadh was merged into the empire of British East India Company. This was a glaring instance of the annihilation of a native state having a glorious history. But the Nawab possessed neither the power nor the resources to put up resistance.

The East India Company started bringing about

drastic changes in the administrative system of Awadh, including Lucknow. The last Nawab was exiled to Calcutta, where he received an annuity of Rs 12 lakh. Before the armed revolt of 1857, Lucknow used to be a prominent city of North India, famous for its grandeur and splendour. The central part of the city was thickly populated and the main roads bustled with commuters and other citizens. Situated at the estuary of the river Gomti, Lucknow's white palatial buildings with their bejewelled domes sparkled from afar. Its delicate-looking minarets soared upwards at various places, adding to the magnificence of the city. These minarets were very high and formed the topic of eager discussions.

In those days, Lucknow ranked as the second largest city in terms of area after Madras (today's Chennai). Although it was not a commercial centre nor enjoyed a reputation for manufacturing and construction activities, it earned fame for its high cultural finesse and opulence.

The tremors of 1857 did not leave Lucknow untouched. The Chief Commissioner of Awadh, Sir Henry Lawrence had taken charge on 20 March 1857, only a few months before the beginning of the uprising on 10 May, in Meerut. In those days, there used to be a British soldier and an officer for every ten Indian soldiers in the army battalions. That would make 700 hundred soldiers of British or European origin for 7,000 men. It would not be an exaggeration to point out that even before Meerut, ripples of armed disturbances had started in Lucknow. This was clear from the incident of burning down the house of a sergeant of the 48 Battalion which took place in April of that year when some remarks concerning the lower caste led to a heated discussion and display of emotions. Sir Henry Lawrence was quick to take steps by raising the walls of the Residency and fortifying the ordnance depot to prevent repetition of such events. There were signs of restlessness on 30 April 1857 concerning the question of cartridges having animal grease, but Sir Henry Lawrence gave a speech in Hindustani to impress upon the Hindus and Muslims the sense of duty towards the Company and tried to convince them that in the eyes of the administration, both Hindus and Muslims were equal. Two days before this address, Meerut had already been rocked by violent rebellion. Soon after the durbar, Sir Lawrence received a telegram informing him of the unusual developments in Meerut. As a resort against any such eventuality, he not only reinforced the defences of Residency but deployed additional forces for its safety and sounded alert all over the places.

Lucknow became engulfed in the fire of uprising on 30 May 1857. The revolutionaries were setting the houses of British officers on fire and retaliated fiercely against whoever came in their way. Lawrence made use of force to push back the recalcitrant men, who fled in the direction of Sitapur, leaving behind a few who received much sympathy and support from the local people.

Due to poor health, Lawrence formed a five-member committee headed by Finance Commissioner Gabins to whom he delegated all power. What happened afterwards is enshrined in the chronicles of a bitter and bloody fight between the champions of freedom and the British forces. In 1902, the name of North-West Province was changed to United Province of Agra and Awadh which popularly came to be called United Provinces or UP. Until then, Allahabad was its capital, but in 1920 it was shifted to Lucknow.

As far as contemporary history is concerned, Liaqat Ali Khan had made up his mind to dedicate himself to the service of society and the country and not indulge in a useless life of luxury in pursuit of wealth and pleasure. That is why he had become avidly interested in political life. A combination of hard work and good luck turned him into a household name. His education imbibed in him a logical perception and an intellectual strength to make a rational assessment and explanation of the social and political realities which were evident in his speeches. Thus, his sober personality earned him a lot of prestige and respect. Though he was a married man, his stay in Oxford and the life he lived after his return had already alienated him from his wife Jehangira Begum to such an extent that they had nothing to do with one another. Yet he saw to it that she and her son led a comfortable life and did not face any trouble on account of paucity of funds or material means till the time they migrated to Pakistan. He bequeathed to Jehangira Begum and their son all the land holdings and *jagirs* located in Karnal and Muzaffarnagar to which they were entitled. This included huge buildings and houses with priceless heirlooms which Liaqat had inherited from his forefathers.

In this uncertain and eventful phase, Irene's coming in contact with him exerted a calming influence on his mind and applied a balm to his frayed emotions. As their intimacy increased, they began to realise that there had grown a unique convergence in their thinking and points of view as though one was made for the other, though circumstances did not appear to favour them. For Irene it was a period of trial; difficulties in her way of marrying Liaqat looked like an unsurpassable barrier. Her own family had adopted a firm, rigid attitude. Her father, Daniel Pant, didn' even want to listen to anything about marriage, nor was he ready to speak a word about it. Perhaps from their viewpoint, this was justified, because the isolation they had suffered at the hands of their clan and society in general even after so many years, symbolised a kind of tangible social boycott, as their religious conversion was considered a social stigma among his people. For this, he could not be blamed. His decision was the outcome of an arduous process of debate and polemical discussions; he chose liberal ways and views of life and rejected conservatism. Now the question of granting permission to one of his daughters to marry into some other religion did not arise, according to his worldview.

Putting aside these vexatious issues, the couple beamed with happiness in the *nikah* ceremony. Their relief and pride were evident on their faces, both appeared to be floating on a cloud of bliss, seeing their dream fulfilled. Nawab Saheb was attired in his expensive *sherwani* and *achkan* and the newly transformed Begum Sahiba, Irene, in her gold-embroidered Lucknowi *kurta-sharara* with a *dupatta* (long scarf) that sparkled with richly embroidered patterns. That dream had attained its much-awaited goal after a long and painful wait.

Somehow, relationships tend to shed their aura soon and emerge in their stark character. The beauty that one perceives in them earlier is no longer seen and its place is taken by irritable day-to-day tussle, bickering and tension. Ego takes the upper hand and erodes all the beauty and sweetness of living together. Even when one tries to improve things, the time that is gone never returns, try as much as one may. But this relationship was gaining greater strength with time and becoming sweeter. Truly, they appeared to be made for each other. It was seen as an example for others, a model to be followed by those in search of stability and charm in a romantic bond.

After the *nikah*, Liaqat and Ra'ana Begum left for Nainital to spend their early tender days of togetherness at the invitation of the Governor of United Provinces, Nawab Chhatri. People wondered at the perfect match the couple symbolised, whose very presence in one another's company seemed to enliven the surroundings. It seemed that one flowed and fused into the other in what can only be described as divine chemistry, which inspired them to live each moment of their life to the fullest. It is this thirst for life which brought them closer in complete surrender of the self, not for a day but an endless journey till their last breath.

Both suffered losses which they must have anticipated in bringing about this marriage. At their wedding many of the traditional ideas were ignored, those notions which not only challenged the bride and bridegroom but raised questions about the two families and social sanctions. It also meant that she never again visited Almora, her place of birth, where she had learned to toddle and walk, and confronted most of life's ups and downs standing by her family.

The person who came under the impact of this development most of all was Irene's father Daniel Pant. He never imagined that the liberal education, freedom of individual opinion and choice and the modern spirit of their adopted religion would bear such fruits that he would hardly be able to raise his head in the bourgeois society he lived in. Her mother too began to show signs of the considerable strain she experienced inside, and the cracks began to show. She could come up with no possible explanation of this act of Irene to cast aside her identity. Her baptism into Christianity had been the most significant event which Daniel had inscribed in the family copy of the Bible; because for him, baptism of every child was of utmost importance. There is no doubt that Irene had been provided such a family atmosphere wherein she learned to be self-dependent and was encouraged to make her own decisions. Against this background, if her decision regarding marriage was contrary to the expectations of the family elders, no one could grudge it.

People noticed a striking similarity between the marital life of Liaqat Ali Khan and his political guru and ideal, Muhammad Ali Jinnah. The spouses of both carried influences of modern outlook, were younger than them, belonged to a different religion and had consented to adopt Islam after marriage. Here, however, the parallel ended. Jinnah's marriage ran into rough weather soon enough. He, a man of forty years, fell in love with a sixteen-year-old Parsi girl whose father, Dinshaw Petit had a flourishing business. It was not unnatural for a father to object to such an affair and marriage. It did not matter to him whether by then Jinnah had become a successful barrister and had carved for himself a top position in the country's freedom movement.

That love does not obey logic was true in the case of Rattanbai and Jinnah. Defying her father's strong objection, Ruttie entered into *nikah* with Jinnah as soon as she turned eighteen. They presented a charming picture of an ideally compatible couple. Anyone setting eyes on them felt overwhelmed by their extraordinary, almost other-worldly lure. In popular opinion, they combined scholarly sobriety with a fashionable inclination towards the good things of life. Jinnah was slim, imposing and poised, possessing such facial features as would attract anyone. He could mesmerise his audience by his amazing oratory. Ruttie was a family girl, delicate in physique, wrapped up in beautiful dreams of a life filled with tender love and emotional well-being. She hardly understood the meaning of married life when a serious responsibility of fulfilling the dream of her love came to rest on her shoulders. Slowly, she came to realise what an incompatible love it was. Ruttie's love was a teenage girl's infatuation, exuberant and flighty, not the deep and serious love looking for a firm anchor in life. Immature as she was, she looked upon Jinnah as a classmate in the same age group, often treating him in her childish, flirtatious playfulness to teasing and girlish pranks which reduced such a sombre-looking politician to a mere child, at her mercy.

This couldn't have continued for long. Jinnah was not destined to be both a lover and a politician at the same time. Love demanded total submission, oblivious to everything else. How was that possible? The country was passing through a political phase on which Jinnah needed to focus all his efforts and attention—his profession also drew his energy to its complex demands. Other priorities and inclinations that age puts on a person combined to distance him from Ruttie. She felt it acutely, her loneliness, and his drifting away from her. She tried hard to mend the relationship, but the more she tried, the more the gulf between them increased. The void in her life became darker and deeper. A spirit of dejection settled over her and she never again became that giggling, agile and playful girl she had once been.

No one can be held responsible for this state of affairs. It takes a long time for relationships to mature. Love needs to be cultivated with patience over a long period. Jinnah could not dive deep into Ruttie's heart and settle there with all the love he was capable of. Though he wanted very much to give time to her, he just couldn't do so. She had everything to make her life comfortable, all the conveniences and facilities to keep her busy in elite social circles, but the more Jinnah plunged into his political and social activities, the further she remained from his concerns and interests. Her loneliness cast a deadly shadow on her life. Suddenly she was decimated by the clutches of death. Jinnah was shaken into a realisation of where he had erred, but by then it was too late. Ruttanbai Jinnah was beyond succour and recall.

Liaqat Ali Khan's case was very different. His love for Ra'ana was boundless. Both were complementary to each other in the fullest sense of the term. Begum Ra'ana made it a point to engage in her husband's every activity. This produced two results: Their life was consistently illuminated by the radiance of their being together, and they were in a position to give the best hours of their time to one another. Their love found space to nourish their relationship as they kept working in unison; it grew into a spiritual urge that each felt for the other. They continued to savour the heady flavour of their love while remaining busy in external matters. Nothing came in their way, neither their age nor anything else. The couple got invitations to many gatherings—their arrival was like the blowing of a fresh breeze laden with perfume. Even the British could not repress their admiration for this well-dressed, impressive pair regarded as an ideal newly married couple.

It is said that history takes notice of one when one performs something out of the ordinary. It is for such people that history takes up the pen and begins a chronicle. Irene's marriage was not an everyday occurrence. It was an extraordinary event—it was an expression of that supreme quality which was first seen in Babu Tara Dutt Pant, the courage to adopt an unknown religion. Something of that heroic courage was seen in Liaqat Ali. He had all the means available for spending a life of unending luxury and comfort like a prince, but he chose to plunge into a struggle for liberating the country from the clutches of colonialist rulers, knowing full well the extreme hardships it entailed. He showed his fighting spirit in overstepping traditionalist thinking to marry Irene.

Once someone asked Irene what exceptional quality she saw in Liaqat Ali which made her decide to tie her fate with him. Her answer: 'His simplicity and honesty.'

In her opinion, one must stand by one's convictions and keep the fire of zeal ever burning. She saw to it that ample time was given to test their love. He never gave her any occasion to complain about anything. A second factor was her deep interest in social work. From early years, she began to take a close look at the life and problems of the lower class of society and felt an urge to work for their betterment. Now she had the company and support of Liaqat, which gave her an elevated sense of assurance.

In Almora, she would go to the hospital to serve the ailing patients and to prisoners serving out their sentence, bringing to them great relief and joy. This is what made

Irene so different from other children of her age. It was in her nature to give attention to the difficulties of life and find a solution to them. She was lovingly called 'Chhoti Bulbul' (Small Nightingale). Despite heavy-weight social and political commitments, it is not that the couple ignored or considered the material-physical pleasures as running contrary to their noble efforts and goals.

This was the time when the capital of British India was being transferred from Calcutta to Delhi. New Delhi was gearing up for its new responsibilities; magnificent buildings were rearing up in their majestic aura on Raisina Hills to house new government offices and departments. The celebrated British architects Sir Edwin Lutyens and Herbert Baker laid the foundation of this orderly new city just adjacent to the chaotically proliferating old Shahjehanabad with its constricted streets, narrow lanes, big palaces rubbing shoulders with a growing tangle of smaller residential houses and teeming market places of jewellery, spices, cloth, and sundry other things. This couldn't have offered a decent setting for administrative work. New Delhi was declared the empire's new capital barely two years before Irene's wedding.

They made their home at 8-B Hardinge Avenue, today's Tilak Marg. A decent bungalow in that locality today will cost a whopping sum of money. Irene and Liaqat gave such a facelift to this house that every nook and corner exuded vibrations of their love for it. There would be constant arrival of visitors, each one of whom received open-armed hospitality which soon became the main topic of public discussions. The most memorable event in that house was the banquet they lavished on certain chosen visitors.

Music became a significant component of their domestic life. Liaqat himself had been trained in the vocal, and could impressively play piano and *tabla* whose heavenly notes filled the house almost the whole day. Begum Ra'ana was not far behind. She could not only play the piano and guitar but sing very well. Their private musical sittings always had a small crowd of appreciators who were surprised to see both perform with such rare mastery and full involvement. They used to sing English and Indian songs to the great amusement of the visitors. Husband and wife would sit down to play bridge and chess, feeling that they were transported to a paradise where time had nearly stopped.

The idea of establishing a new city called New Delhi as the grand new capital of British India was mooted by King George V when he came to attend Delhi Durbar with his wife in 1911. This part of Delhi had been in the past the arena of mighty dynasties such as the great Hindu Kings, Muslim Sultans, Lodhis and Mughals, steeped as they had been in bloodshed and untold sorrows which constant warfare brings in its trail, as well as celebrating periods of great victory and pride. Delhi witnessed many phases of its rise and decline.

It is not true that most of the time Irene and Liaqat immersed themselves in the pleasures and fun of married life, for a major part of their day was occupied by their social and political engagements. Yet whatever time he could spare for Irene, small though it was, or Irene could devote to him, revealed the pure sense of complete submission of one to the other and intensity of their feelings. This is possible when two lovers have perfect chemistry that draws them together, and their vastly different cultures and faiths don't come in their way or are not allowed to come.

It is during this time, when they had settled down in their house, 'Gul-e-Ra'ana' at 8-B Hardinge Avenue, that Muhammad Ali Jinnah emerged as a prominent name in the country's freedom movement. Having participated in many agitations, he had become an undisputed supporter of self-rule. Jinnah used to be a frequent visitor to the home of the Liaqat couple where he was treated to fantastic dinners—he loved good food and lively discussions. He was also actively associated with the All India Home Rule League which was established in 1916 by Annie Besant and Bal Gangadhar Tilak. Initially, he was inclined towards the Congress Party.

With time, Jinnah's affiliation with the Muslim League became stronger. In the 1927 and 1928 Conventions, he was elected permanent President of the League; however, he continued to be a member of the Congress Party where he used to plead for Hindu-Muslim unity. But soon Mahatma Gandhi's hold over Congress became firm and the differences in the thinking of both came out in the open. These differences grew so sharp that Jinnah thought it prudent to part ways with Congress.

When in 1928 the Simon Commission visited India, it was decided that Jinnah would lead Muslim League and Congress protested against its arrival. Liaqat Ali also firmly stood by his leader. He gave very impactful speeches in the Legislative Assembly of the United Provinces. In this scenario of seething discontent and vociferous opposition, Irene and her classmates also contributed their mite in the anti-Simon rallies.

The same year, British Home Secretary Lord Frederick Simon Birkenhead gave a call to prominent Indians, social organisations and political parties to come forward with suggestions for constitutional reforms. Congress Party constituted an all-party Reforms Committee under the chairmanship of Motilal Nehru whose recommendations were squarely dismissed by a majority of the Muslim League members. The party felt that this went against the spirit of the Lucknow resolution which gave greater room to the Muslims. This was the issue that later became the main cause for the complete rift between Jinnah and Congress, and he felt compelled to leave the party. From the League's side, a 14-point document was issued which primarily underlined the need for substantial share to be given to Muslims in the country's politics after India became free.

A stage had by then been reached in the history of India's struggle for freedom when the British rulers had come to realise that their days in the country were numbered and it was not possible to rule it for long. Sooner or later, they must grant freedom to the people or the consequences might be gruesome. But they were quite slow in moving in that direction. They decided to grab the opportunity when they saw that the Hindu-Muslim gulf was widening. Jinnah in those days had been going through depression and a sense of failure. His beautiful wife's death had shaken him badly. A feeling of apathy to worldly things had been growing in him but times were delicate and needed men of action. Besides, pressure from his community was growing on him, compelling him to come out of his cocoon and take the reins once again with renewed vigour. He took up for discussion his 14-point document which was to be presented in the Muslim League convention and which became the chief reason for his differences with the Congress Party. The meeting ran into disorderly scenes and ended without passing a resolution. The already dejected Jinnah received another jolt when the Second Round Table Conference convened by the British Prime Minister Ramsay MacDonald also terminated without coming to any conclusion.

These developments contributed in alienating him from politics and forced his thoughts into contemplating a change in the course of his life. He was extremely disappointed by the constant tussle within the organisation and a continuing state of indecision. Finally, he left for England with his family in 1930. He had some experience of legal practice there—now he had the support of his younger sister Fatima Jinnah. His daughter Dina got admission in a boarding school. The task of managing his home fell to Fatima, who carried that responsibility most efficiently.

In the absence of Jinnah, the leadership of the Muslim League was assigned to Sir Mohammad Iqbal. In 1933, the second frontline Muslim League leader Chowdhary Rehmat Ali conceived the idea of a separate country for Muslims of all shades and affiliations and gave it the name of 'Pakistan'—the pure land. He believed that Indian Muslims would find for themselves a safe and secure land where they can progress unhindered. But was it as simple to attain as it looked? Even the extremist Jinnah never imagined a Muslim country apart from India till that juncture.

The person who took over the reins of Muslim League after a dejected Jinnah left the country's political scene was the celebrated poet and philosopher Iqbal. Mohammad Iqbal's grandfather was a Hindu Kashmiri Pandit who later settled in Sialkot. Iqbal attained worldwide fame for his *'Sare jahaan se achcha Hindostan hamara'* verse which became the national song. Other major works of his include *'Asrar-e-Hind'*, *'Rumuz-e-bekhudi'*, and *'Bag-e-dara'*. His Persian works captured the hearts of his admirers in Iran where he was called 'Iqbal-e-Lahore.' He had a doctorate in Philosophy and wrote many philosophical works.

'Tahrir-e-Milli' or community song represents Mohammad Iqbal's homage to Muslim *ummah* or collectivity, imparting his view that in Islam nationalism has no place. In his opinion, wherever Muslims live they are one community, or to use modern parlance,

'one nation'. The leader of the 'nation' is Prophet Mohammad. This is reflected in his poetic line *'Cheen-o-Arab hamara, Hindostan hamara; Muslim hain watan hai, sara jahaan hamara'*, which occurs in *'Tarana-e-Milli'*! Before Partition, Iqbal composed *'Tarana-e-Hind'* which opened with the words, *'Saare jahaan se achcha Hindostan hamara'*. It carried a message for the people of undivided India. In this song he addressed people of different religions as *'Hindi hain hum'*, calling on all to adopt nationalism and patriotism.

Afterwards he, and not Jinnah, came to be regarded as the originator of Pakistan because Iqbal advocated the idea of including Punjab, Sindh, North-West Frontiers and Baluchistan into one exclusive Muslim nation. He was the first person to do so. He put forth this concept of accession in the 21 Conference of Indian Muslim League on 29 December 1930 at Allahabad. It was Iqbal who first raised the question of India's Partition and the creation of Pakistan. Iqbal was the architect of Pakistan which was to be put together by breaking off from India. He invited Muhammad Ali Jinnah to join the Pakistan movement. Though it was to Iqbal that leadership of the Muslim League had fallen, he considered Jinnah as the most suitable leader. In this context, Iqbal's influence on Jinnah was significant. He and Liaqat Ali Khan goaded Jinnah to come out of his self-imposed exile in London and return to India to reactivate Muslim League politics. Before Iqbal's death in 1938, he succeeded in turning Jinnah's political orientation to his ideology and line of action. According to Ahmed, Jinnah fully agreed with Iqbal's views expressed in his letter and communications that India's Muslims needed a separate nation. In 1933, Chowdhary Rehmat Ali presented a detailed explanation of the term 'Pakistan'. He clarified that each letter represents a separate province in South Asia: Punjab, Afghania, Kashmir, Sindh and Baluchistan. Such a combination was looked upon with some doubt by other Muslim leaders, for they feared that justice to all Muslims would not be possible in such a conglomerate state. They still didn't have a charismatic leader of Jinnah's calibre who would be capable of keeping large masses united in hope. The void left by Jinnah was difficult to fill.

At Home with Jinnah

In the meanwhile, there came an opportunity to break the deadlock. Liaqat Ali Khan was summoned to London to present his case before a Joint Judicial Commission. He was newly married and apparently couldn't think of leaving his bride Begum Gul-e-Ra'ana behind. It was arranged that the couple would go to London on honeymoon, but finding political questions and problems demanding immediate attention as a matter of utmost importance, Liaqat couldn't have considered the trip as just a holiday. Nor did Ra'ana Begum see it as all that important in her life. All her energy was absorbed in her husband's monumental endeavour to improve the lot of his countrymen and make a pivotal contribution to the freedom movement. Later, the same energy was directed to the creation of Pakistan and history records their efforts as milestone work. Begum Ra'ana left no stone unturned in persuading Jinnah to return to India and take up the leadership of Muslim League. The records of all these efforts and activities, including the newly married couple's England tour, their meeting with Jinnah and many other incidents are still preserved. Especially notable is Begum Ra'ana's transition from a completely distinct cultural background to creating a space for herself in these male domains and achieving an amazing level of success. In her memoirs, she wrote:

Liaqat and I arrived in London. We met Jinnah at a reception. Without losing time Liaqat requested Jinnah to return to the country. I remember he had said that he needed someone who couldn't be bought. My husband liked this phrase, and he knew that Jinnah couldn't be purchased. Jinnah listened to him, and for a while kept quiet. He narrated something about his life in England and made it clear that he was leading a contented life in Hampshire. But Liaqat had decided that he would not lose heart.

'There is no question of not going to India! You must come. People need you. Only you can put a new life in League and save it from falling apart.'

Perhaps Jinnah was in a good mood that day; who doesn't love to hear sweet words of praise? When Liaqat's adulations were over, he said, 'Both of you are cordially invited to my Hampstead home for dinner tonight. Don't forget. We will discuss everything in detail there.'

It was a beautiful evening. His house looked like a huge stately dwelling with its sprawling lawns and fruit trees laden with fresh apples and other fruits. The atmosphere was enlivened with the sweet chirpings of various kinds of birds whose melodious notes floated all over the place carried by gentle breezes. Miss Fatima Jinnah knew how to take care of every single aspect about the entire arrangement and management of our evening visit. That's why at a point I felt that it was close to impossible to rescue Jinnah from the well-fortified house.

After dinner, Liaqat repeated his appeal to Jinnah. He said that he liked the 'Muslim Jinnah', and that's whom he needed. Ra'ana Begum supported him and said, 'Jinnah Saheb, since long I held you in great worship as a hero. I'm a woman who had been associated with my peer group and in the Muslim League, I can do my job very well. Women must be included in the League in large numbers and I'm sure I can do the job quite easily to make it broader and stronger.'

'You are very young and lack the necessary experience. You do not understand the nature of women nor do you know much about this world,' Jinnah shot back, mincing no words. Despite his position, Jinnah listened to all the arguments. He took a sincere interest and also put forth questions concerning the subject discussed. Liaqat tried to satisfy Jinnah to the best of his ability. Finally, what he said to Liaqat is this, 'You'd better go back to review the scene and make a correct assessment of the sentiments of people hailing from different parts of the country. I will rely on your appraisal and conclusion drawn from it. Even after that if you ask me to return, I shall certainly give up this country and return.'

Jinnah's words stirred a great hope in Liaqat which he clung on to. Liaqat had achieved more than what he had hoped for; his pleased spirit broke out into blissful song which he kept humming.

Begum Ra'ana notes, 'In this mood, we set sail for India. Upon embarking in the country Liaqat had his time excessively occupied with the things done in this tour and related matters. I swear that I've not seen in my entire life such a person as Liaqat who is not satisfied till he dives to the bottom of a task which he takes in hand to probe as thoroughly as his abilities can be stretched. That shows his deep dedication to his work. With a thorough-going approach, he contributes his time to every single person to scrutinise him who is in some way concerned with the matter and could affect it, however remotely. The numbers of such individuals must have gone into thousands…When he was fully satisfied, he sent a message to Jinnah Saheb, "Come now!"'

Irene turned Gul-e-Ra'ana, the wife of Liaqat Ali Khan, was not only devoted to her husband but always participated wholeheartedly in his projects and programmes. After Partition, she put her efforts into providing relief to the displaced refugees. Her heart went out in full sympathy to the Hindu and Muslim women's pitiable plight in refugee camps and she did whatever she could to bring comfort to them. At the same time, she sought to bring Muslim women who kept themselves concealed behind the traditional veil, out of their anonymous life and awakened in them the urge to work for humanity.

Liaqat Ali ensured Jinnah's return, though in the meantime a lot of valuable time had been lost. It was 1935; by the time he made up his mind, two precious years had almost been wasted. It can only be surmised that if Jinnah had stayed on in India, Partition would have acquired a different form since there would be sufficient time to understand the other dimension of the issue, new strategies would have been devised and a new goal would have been reached. But developments took place so fast that conditions no longer existed for any kind of planning.

Jinnah sold his Hampstead house before leaving for India and arrived here to a rousing welcome. Liaqat and Gul-e-Ra'ana had been able to rekindle in his heart the great love for their country which persuaded him to agree to come back. This was despite the fact that he was doing quite well in his profession in England, living a princely life and basking in fame and limelight.

Having come to India, Jinnah needed to set his own affairs in order. He had a house in Bombay but circumstances required that he continuously stay in Delhi and be available to others. Thus started his search for a residence for himself in Delhi. But till then he and Fatima remained the guests of Gul-e-Ra'ana. She saw to it that all his needs were promptly attended to. Jinnah's famous love for sumptuous food became his hosts' central interest. He enjoyed to his heart's content the delicious dishes which were readily served to him, especially by Ra'ana Begum. On a political level, Jinnah found that his ideas and views and those of Liaqat had a striking similarity. He was much impressed by Liaqat's personality, convinced that he had found a reliable friend in him.

Begum Ra'ana writes, 'Jinnah Saheb was crazy about guavas. It was, therefore, made sure that whenever he was invited to meals, there should be guava or dishes made of it.' He had a scientific reason for preferring guava: he believed that it cleanses the human body of toxins, which is why the fruit formed an important part of his diet.

Jinnah used to visit Delhi quite often before 1940 also and stayed at the Imperial Hotel at Janpath which was magnificent enough to cater to his refined tastes and style. Though Jinnah's name is more closely associated with Bombay than Delhi, he spent a good five years (1940-45) in Delhi. His sister Fatima kept close to him and managed his day-to-day life. Much credit goes to her for helping him come out of the state of depression into which he had slid after his wife's death and restoring normalcy to some degree.

In 1939, he decided to build a house for himself as he could not always stay at the residence of Gul-e-Ra'ana or in hotels. So he began to search for a bungalow. After a prolonged hunt, a beautiful bungalow built on a 1.5-acre plot at 10, Aurangzeb Marg, now APJ Abdul Kalam Road, was selected. This two-storey house was designed by Robert Tore Russel, a member of the team of Edward Lutyens who was also involved in designing Connaught Place. Today the Embassy of the Netherlands is located in that house.

Among Jinnah's non-political friends in Delhi were Sardar Sobha Singh (father of the writer Khushwant Singh) and industrialist Seth Ramkrishna Dalmia. The latter's daughter Nilima Dalmia, author of *The Secret Diary* of *Kasturba*, wrote:

'Jinnah talked only of investment and money with my father. He worshipped money. Both had close relations. Jinnah used to visit us very often and regularly in our bungalows at Akbar Road and Sikandra Road.'

Before leaving Delhi forever, Dalmia invited Jinnah for dinner at his residence. His dentist sister Fatima accompanied him. Dalmia's wife Nandini was in command of household duties. Nandini tells us that the atmosphere had become sentimental since Jinnah was to leave Delhi the next day. Despite the hot weather, Jinnah donned a *sherwani* for the flight, whereas normally he used to wear a suit. Among those who had gathered at the airport to see him off stood Dalmia. This was on 7 August 1947, when Jinnah with his sister flew off to

Karachi in Viceroy Lord Mountbatten's plane.

Before departing for Pakistan, Jinnah sold his bungalow to Dalmia for Rs 2.5 lakh. Though they were close friends, Jinnah was not ready to give any concession to him, not even a paisa less. The house had five bedrooms, a huge drawing room, a meeting room and bar. Today its value is estimated at Rs 800 crore. In matters of religion, these close friends stuck firmly to their orthodox points of views. Having acquired Jinnah's house, Dalmia saw to it that the building was 'purified' with Ganga water and the flag that used to flutter atop was taken down and was replaced by the flag of Cow Protection Movement or *Gau Raksha Andolan*. It was in Dalmia's possession until 1964. After that, he sold it to the government of Netherlands, which converted it into the residence of its Ambassador.

Amid these engagements which left little time for the young couple for themselves, Liaqat and Begum Ra'ana managed to reserve some sentimental moments for themselves. They knew how to live life to the fullest. They would move out in pouring rain or visit a tranquil sunset place or just have an intimate evening, lost in a world of their imagination. When necessary, they would shield one another against possible danger.

Shadows began to darken and thicken over the country, but the couple's commitment to its welfare and urge to put everything in its service remained as strong as ever. Soon Liaqat became the father of two sons. Begum Ra'ana had an added responsibility to which she turned all her attention, while Liaqat toured the entire country to consolidate the base of Muslim League and expand its influence. These were days when fear and distrust marked the approach of the two major communities to each other and the political course took a risky turn. Everyone was cautious, alert and wary of others.

The question of self-rule appeared to be resolving itself. But it was not so easy to understand the intentions of the administrators. In the year of the Silver Jubilee of King George V, the Governor of Agra and Awadh conferred state honours on Annie, mother of Begum Ra'ana, for the social services she had rendered. This was considered a very special honour. For the family, there was a particular reason to feel proud. Later in December 1946, the Commissioner of Kumaon also pronounced a regional award to Annie. Her work was so prominent that it couldn't be overlooked. But everyone saw that in addition to this her father Daniel Pant was also a recipient of the title Rai Saheb which showed the administration's good opinion of the family. At first sight, it also appears a result of the good work done by Daniel, especially such matters as pleased the British administration.

There is an interesting anecdote concerning Irene's sympathetic relation with her household staff. There was an old servant in the family named Kishan Singh. This was the time when the news of Irene's marriage had come to be known to all. Kishan Singh used to take care of Irene, the child, and used to call her 'Irene Baba' and she would take food only from his hand. One day in great desperation he contacted Irene alias Begum Ra'ana informing her that his son had disappeared in Bombay. A heart-broken Kishan Singh was searching frantically for his lost son. As soon as she got the message, all available resources were put into action by Begum Ra'ana to trace him. He was also given a bicycle and some financial help. This is how she got a chance to pay back the little debt that she believed she owed to him for taking care of her so well in those happy childhood days. It could not be known whether old man Kishan Singh's son was found or not, but his very arrival filled her heart with contentment as though one of her relatives had come to meet her at a time when her mother, brother and other dear ones had cut themselves off from her after her marriage. They never went to Delhi to meet her nor could she go to Almora to share old memories. One can see that this offered a ready opportunity to some narrow-minded people in society to spin a fantastic yarn about Irene and her wedding and circulate it in Almora. Speculation was rife whether Liaqat Ali and Irene would again come to her Almora house to bring the joys that had fled from its heart, and whether they would be permitted to do so. But nothing of the sort happened as long as they lived, which would further have stoked the fire.

On the political scene of India, Liaqat Ali Khan rose and began to shine with amazing rapidity like a new-found star by dint of his zeal and will power, as well as the extraordinary support given by his Begum. In times of great disturbance and turmoil, the strategy of the couple was proving to be effective. In 1936, Jinnah proposed the name of Liaqat Ali Khan for the post of General Secretary of the Muslim League. He was elected unanimously. The pressure of work was increasing day by day, but he also had the assurance of his wife's presence by his side. Her wholehearted support for his work made the political journey smooth. On one hand, he kept himself busy in all kinds of questions concerning the country and the party, on the other, his wife grappled with domestic problems and turned their home into a haven of peace and comfort. To handle a large amount of correspondence she learned to type, for the party did not have enough funds to maintain either a professional typist regularly or an office for its systematic functioning. To lag behind in these politically volatile times could prove fatal. Begum Ra'ana did all the work of an office secretary for her husband. There was another person to assist her, ready to do anything for the sake of the party, a spirit of self-denial that was urgently needed at the time.

New Delhi was taking on a new look under the supervision of the designer Edward Lutyens. New buildings meant for all purposes had begun to spring up: large government offices, departments, residences and markets, so different from the more familiar unplanned city of Shahjehanabad with its disorderly growth. New Delhi caught the breath of onlookers with its modern architectural grandeur and immaculately designed layout. Even today we can see it in its undisturbed expansive appearance. From 1920 to 1924, the work of constructing this new city continued. It became the centre of activities of Begum Ra'ana and Liaqat Ali Khan. The contribution of Sir Lutyen in shaping modern New Delhi to make it a suitable place as the central government's administrative outfit remains unparalleled. The Viceroy House, now Rashtrapati Bhawan, catches the eye of anyone visiting the city with its regal majesty radiating from every corner.

Delhi, reeling under the hot sun, has never been a comfortable place to live in the months of summer. People used to go to hill stations like Shimla, Nainital, Mussoorie every year to seek a more pleasant climate. Both Liaqat and Ra'ana also used to make sorties to the hills to escape the torturous heat and come back with renewed vigour.

During one such spell of hot weather, the couple experienced the unexpected joy of living together amidst nature's munificence in Shimla. In 1937, both had been staying in the Cassis Hotel for a long, comfort-filled duration. Ra'ana had given birth to a son on 3 October. His birth brought to Liaqat much joy and busier days. That year from May to September-end, Liaqat had so much on his hands that besides Delhi, Lucknow and Shimla he was called upon to visit London also. Little Ashraf (that was the name of the newborn) needed his parent's attention. Begum Ra'ana lavished on him all the love and attention he required while Liaqat didn't allow himself to be overburdened with unnecessary sentiments. But whenever he could find the time, he would spend it with his infant.

It was Muhammad Ali Jinnah who gave Liaqat's son

the name Ashraf. The parents wanted to call him Akbar, but when they saw that Jinnah had other ideas, they didn't object. Four years later, when on 10 April 1941 a second son was born to them, their wish to name their child Akbar was fulfilled.

Mother, Wife and Policymaker

When Ra'ana Begum was Irene, she displayed a unique motherly instinct towards her younger brother and sisters. She enjoyed bringing orderliness in their chaotic, noisy lives, picking up their scattered belongings, resolving their quarrels, sharing their pleasures and problems and lending the house a positive aura. The same disposition was seen in the application of her emotional and disciplinarian approach to her husband and house. Her sole objective in doing so was to see the light of joy on their faces, and she became successful in doing so. No one could claim that they saw any quarrel or dispute in Liaqat's family. There was an intense sense of commitment and devotion to whatever she did. In this connection her friend Kay Miles writes:

Despite her busy programmes and responsibilities she gave time to her family which it needed. She kept a close eye on every family member's personal needs, education and day to day exigencies. Liaqat, being deeply immersed in his eventful political routine, could not give time to his family; in such a situation, Ra'ana Begum acted as both mother and father to their children. They got a mother's love and father's lessons in stern discipline from her alone.

We all know how wealthy family's children are brought up; from those days to our time there has hardly occurred any change. Money is spent indiscriminately on them to get all the conveniences of life, most of which are not really needed. Their childhood is spent in the company of servants and *ayahs* and education is obtained through tutors who see to it that they get promoted to the next class. But Begum Ra'ana had planned to impart all the values of life to her children herself. She was clear in her head about her role in bringing them up in an ideal manner. Her determination found ample support in Liaqat's endorsement of her endeavours and whenever it became possible, he himself engaged actively in this project.

What Begum Ra'ana wished to inculcate in both her children and succeeded in doing so was punctuality or great regard for time. There has to be, she told them, a proper balance between time and one's work; both should be tailored to fit into one another. This must be reflected in one's day-to-day living. She also told them about the significance of modesty and decency which she valued as the second most important attribute. She believed that sobriety plays a vital role in one's success in life, equal only to dedication and passionate submission. Work done with excellent efficiency but without modesty and sobriety may fail to leave an agreeable impression. The children were also told to respect others' feelings. These are the traits which Liaqat and Ra'ana Begum had done their best to imbibe in their life. She would supervise her children's homework rather than leave it to the care of the tutor. She understood the value of involvement with children as creating a profound bond with them. She kept track of their smallest acts and conduct in school and provided them with the necessary guidance when required.

Muhammad Ali Jinnah used to come to 'Gul-e-Ra'ana' often. The friends would relax playing bridge or holding leisurely conversations. Children were instructed to greet Jinnah with the traditional *'Aadab'* and withdraw when the adults got down to chatting or a game of cards. The close relationship which developed between Jinnah and Liaqat families is indicated by their eager wait for the summer holidays when they used to visit Kashmir and spend fabulous time in houseboats. During this period, children were placed under strict instruction to behave in a manner that would not upset Jinnah's privacy. Besides maintaining a firm code of conduct, children were also told to follow specific dress codes.

There was hardly a hot season when the two families

didn't visit Kashmir. This trip undertaken in the car was full of thrill and the pleasure of sight-seeing. The excitement of children, the delight of going on a long drive, the ebullience of watching punctured wheels being changed—all this contributed to the joy of their summer vacations. Another notable point is that more than the driver, Nawab Saheb was a good hand at changing punctured tyres; he had far better technical knowledge about cars than the driver. Tinkering with cars and learning about their finer technical aspects were his hobbies. He had a deep interest in improving the automobile and keeping it in consistently good condition.

All said Liaqat, Ra'ana Begum, Ashraf and Akbar were leading a contented life of pleasure-filled, purposeful activities. They were a shining example of what a family should be like with affectionate bonds, nurturing high values of life and often used to become a topic of discussion among the intelligentsia and the elite. It is not unusual to find any individual with some peculiar habit which sets him apart from others. It cannot be explained by the application of logic or reasoning or by any other convincing argument. It is just there in him. Liaqat was a smoker, but he kept his habit strictly within the limits. He was not a chain smoker. However, he possessed an inordinate interest in collecting lighters, to such an extent that he was second to none in this matter. Wherever he went, if he spotted a new lighter, he would add it to his fabulous collection. It became his singular obsession. It was the job of Begum Ra'ana to keep the large lighter collection in order, which she did with great pleasure. When after Partition he chose to make Pakistan his home, there was among his belongings a huge suitcase with an enormous variety of lighters.

One of his other hobbies was photography. Though in Europe and America, particularly in Germany photography had gained much advancement, the transfer of technology here was much slower in those days compared to our times. Much of the 'developed' technology would come to India when it became obsolete in Europe. Using a camera required much time and patience. But having a deep love for it, Liaqat would always be on the lookout for the best cameras available, take photos of his wife and children and admire the effect. He had learned the technique of developing negatives in the darkroom and achieved a good level of expertise. It is because of this hobby that today we have a good pictorial account of the journey of Muslim League which was abundantly photographed by him at every stage of its growth. Even historian Roger Lang mentions it in his memoirs.

Ra'ana Begum indeed used to lead a life of luxury in keeping with her husband's status and capabilities, but the essential qualities of sobriety and humility never diminished in both. She lived a well-ordered, tidy life, and liked to dress elegantly. But she was not an exhibitionist like other women of her class, and certainly didn't like to put her jewellery on display. In an interview, she said:

'I do not have any interest in anything that conspires

to turn me into an idle, comfortably placed person. There is nothing better than to live life as it comes to you.'

The only perfume she loved to wear was called 'Joy'! It can't be said that she had a specific signature style which was instantly identified with Begum Ra'ana.

In the matter of colours, her favourite was pastel green; whether for garments or selection of tapestry for her home, her eyes would naturally rivet on this shade only. It was a pleasant coincidence that this was also Liaqat's favourite shade. There couldn't be a happier thing for a married couple than to discover such common tastes in the matter of house decoration. As for her temper, Begum Ra'ana herself admitted that sometimes she used to lose her cool and fly into a rage, but Liaqat never allowed even a wrinkle to disturb the equanimity of his face, which became a greater reason for her to become angrier. His gentle smile would finally cool the heat of her fury in a happy resolution. Their emotional debates were not allowed to become a topic of social-political gossip among common people. That's what made their relationship so attractive.

Like his political mentor Muhammad Ali Jinnah, and contrary to British rulers' approach, at least initially, Liaqat was a staunch supporter of Hindu-Muslim amity and fraternity. The change which occurred later on, was due to social and political conditions. Begum Ra'ana's presence did much to create a balance and maintain it. Her Kumaoni Brahmin values remained intact even after her father adopted Christianity. The couple would often get involved in heated debates with Dharma Veer, who hailed from Bijnor district of UP. After completing his education from Muir College of Allahabad he went to London where he earned a great reputation as an Orientalist and an authority on Oriental Studies and cleared the Indian Civil Services exam. He was the only top bureaucrat who was honoured not only by India's first Prime Minister but also by the first Prime Minister of Pakistan and became a reliable confidant of both. He writes in his memoirs:

> Liaqat Ali Khan also like Jinnah had emerged as a prominent and staunch nationalist leader in the early years. I find no reason to disbelieve that had the top leaders' behaviour towards him been one of honesty, the subsequent political and communal developments would not have led to partition.

It is also said that once the frontline Congress leader of Almora, Pandit Govind Vallabh Pant, who was himself a Kumaoni Brahmin, tried to include Liaqat in the party, but for some reason, the latter turned down the offer. Perhaps it was too late by then. Disruption of communal harmony which set in with the dawn of the 1940s was a rude shock to all. Worst affected was the United Provinces and nearby areas. This led to a widening of the rift between the Congress and the Muslim League that could never be bridged. A natural consequence of this was that Liaqat Ali emerged as a leader who provoked the sentiments of the Muslim community. It was seen for the first time on 24 February 1939 when he targeted the government in UP Assembly on the question of communal conflicts. He came up as the spokesperson of Muslim sentiments. In politics, friendships last as long as they serve one's interests. Liaqat wished to draw a line. Here are some excerpts from his address:

> Sir,
>
> The address of the honourable leader of the house is a testament to his frustration and desperation. Can I appeal to the honourable member to look for the cause of the communal bitterness that prevails in this province, around his own house? The speech of Vijay Pal Singh reflects the attitude of the Congress workers towards the minorities. Why can't you understand that not everyone from amongst you is like you or Jawaharlal ji? Why can't you understand that there are within you many who show themselves great nationalists but in truth are die-hard communalists of the lowest category? My respected friend Vijay Pal Singh said that he has a solution for the problem. He said that if the two communities want to solve their problem by fighting each other then why not let them fight and find a solution? Would he like to say the same regarding the North-West Frontier Province? Will this apply to Sindh also?
>
> He has suggested this remedy for the province where the percentage of the population of his community is 86 per cent. Is that the only answer

left for such a lot of questions? I'd like to say, and say it with a full sense of responsibility that it is this mentality that has taken grip of the Congress people, and which is also responsible for the sour relations that exist between the two communities. Sir, the point is whether the government should understand that, forgetting its background, it should not consider itself great nationalist, be it in villages or districts. That's the reason why popular trust in the Party has weakened. (Interruptions, noise).

This friend of mine has raised all kinds of questions and will continue to do so. But there is no difference in the mentality of Congressmen and the members of Hindu Mahasabha. Sir, is it not the duty of the majority to create a feeling of trust in the minority? I talk of the Muslims among the minority; they constitute only 14 per cent. This province wants to live in peace. It knows the meaning of fighting, which is nothing but an easy way to self-destruct…if a few Congress people who constitute not more than one per cent of the total population, consider themselves so strong that they can drive the British out of the country, then let it be clear that they cannot suppress 11 crore Muslims of the country so easily. They are determined to lead a respectable life despite what you say and what you do.

It is my suggestion that you change your mindset

and live with better thinking. Sir, this respected member can interrupt my speech...but the more he tries to disrupt my words the more pleased I shall be, for that would assure me that my points are making dents in their minds. They also know that what I say has truth in it. How is it that in other states communal hostilities are not as strong as they are here? Can it be said that in Punjab or Sindh or Bengal or North-West Frontier regions communal feelings are not so intense? (One voice: 'Because the Muslim League has failed there'). No, it is not that. It is so because in these provinces the government did not show favour to any political party. That is the reason, if the government wants to command people's trust, it should rise above party affiliations to generate a sense of safety in their minds and assume that all would get equal justice and not only Congress.

The speech demonstrates that Liaqat Ali Khan had created a fair distance from the Congress and drawn up his separate agenda. Later on, towards the last week of March, in a large gathering of Muslim League at Meerut, Liaqat Ali Khan made it clear:

'In the prevailing circumstances, it is meaningless to hope for a better future for the Muslims...I want such an independent India where Muslims wield power and freedom because Muslims constitute a nation, not just a community!'

People had by then come to realise that Partition of the country was inevitable. There would finally come a day when there would be no way out but to accept the two-nation theory—two nations based on followers of two religions: Hindus and Muslims.

It is during these tense days that it appeared that deep inside, Begum Ra'ana disagreed with Liaqat Ali Khan. At the height of these political debates, she took her son Ashraf to Mussoorie, far from the noise and din of the political bickering. She spent the whole period of her stay with Ashraf. She utilised her time in taking the boy into jungles and valleys, telling him about flora and fauna, the geography and culture of the region. Since he could never visit his maternal grandmother in Almora, Begum Ra'ana tried to compensate by taking him to Mussoorie's enchanting landscape. She maintained contact with her husband through letters and telegrams. Events were moving at a fast pace. Every day there were reports of new developments forcing the country on a path which it should have avoided.

And then suddenly there occurred the cataclysmic event of World War II which shook the world for six years. It started in September 1939. So long as Britain did not declare war against Germany, events followed a course much as the world expected. But the day it did, India got involved almost without taking into confidence its people or the elected representatives or its prominent activists. Who knows why Viceroy Lord Linlithgow took such a step? As a natural reaction, there was an uproar of protest in every corner of the country against this insensible action; severe criticism and *en masse* resignations of the representatives of provincial governments. This led to a strange situation of no state having an effective government. But the Muslim leaders tried to take a different stand; thinking they would gain out of the war, they stood in support of Great Britain. Both Jinnah and Liaqat Ali Khan took advantage of the situation as per their convenience. But they were also aware of the feelings of the huge masses of the country, and kept a safe distance from the administration to show their cooperation.

Muhammad Ali Jinnah was at New Delhi's 'Gul-e-Ra'ana' house while Liaqat and Begum Ra'ana were out of the capital on vacation. The Nehru Report brought disillusionment to both the parties regarding the prospect of their joining hands once again and making a concerted effort for building a secular, independent India. Now Muslim League's only agenda was to demand a separate nation for the Muslims.

On 22 March 1940, in the Annual Conference of Muslim League was laid the foundation of a new nation called Pakistan. At that time, Chief Minister of undivided Bengal AK Fazlul Haq openly demanded a separate homeland for Muslims of British India. Chowdhary Khalijumman supported it, presenting all those reasons which in his view made it unavoidable. Full-throated support also came from Moulana Zafar Ali Khan of Punjab, Mohammad Abdul Ghafoor Hazarvi of North-

West Frontier Province, Sir Abdullah Haran of Sindh, Kazi Isa of Balochistan, and others.

Leaders of the Congress by and large staunchly opposed any such demand, but some members appeared to sympathise with it tacitly. One prominent leader said that such an action would be unfortunate but it was also the valid right of India's Muslim community. In these conditions, Muhammad Ali Jinnah and Liaqat Ali Khan had found a steady direction and were moving in that direction to achieve their goal. Their movement had been set in motion.

Liaqat Ali Khan had begun as a provincial leader, having been elected to the State Assembly of UP from Muzaffarnagar. Later, he got into the Central Legislative Assembly (precursor to the Lok Sabha) from Meerut. He was also promoted as the Deputy Leader of Muslim League's Legislative Council. He was visible now on a larger political canvas of the country. On one hand, his residence 'Gul-e-Ra'ana' had become the centre of high political activities, on the other, his wife Ra'ana Begum was preparing herself for the arrival of a second child. Lost in the thoughts of her child's coming, she felt that a discreet distance from politics would be good for her. Even before the birth of Pakistan, her second child Akbar was born. The drawing room of 'Gul-e-Ra'ana' became a place where history was being made. With it, however, her dreams got shattered—she still relished sweet memories of Almora. When Ra'ana Begum was going through the hope-filled birth pangs which signalled Akbar's arrival in the world, her home had become the centre of activities which eventually led to the birth of a new nation. When Ra'ana Begum had begun her labour pain, Liaqat was in Madras in connection with a party campaign. On 10th April 1941, Akbar was born—Liaqat was busy in a series of meetings. On 24 April, the child and mother were discharged from hospital. To escape the strong heat of Delhi the family went away to the hill station, Mussoorie where they stayed till the middle of September. But in the meantime, Liaqat could not avoid returning to work. Jinnah felt that it was quite necessary to bring out a newspaper to reach their ideas to every individual of India's large population. Liaqat agreed with it. Thus, began the publication of the weekly newspaper *The Dawn* on 26 October 1941. Its owner was Muhammad Ali Jinnah, while Liaqat Ali Khan was appointed its Managing Director and Hassan Ahmad its first Editor. Published from Delhi, this English newspaper had a double-edged benefit. Firstly, Liaqat could present his views most effectively to the outside world; secondly, he could give useful political, economic and social messages to his supporters. It was natural that it was considered as the main organ of the League. Priced at two annas, the paper acquired such wide popularity overnight that the editor demanded a salary raise. Jinnah said:

'For the first time, Muslims would be reading a first-class English newspaper, and I'm sure, the people of India would lodge full trust and come out in support of it.'

Experts in Indo-Pak relations agree that this newspaper

played an important role in expanding the contact of the Muslim League with the masses. Eventually, it was instrumental in creating a large, strong public opinion for Pakistan. Time was moving fast and Liaqat too was moving from place to place making busy rounds of all kinds of engagements. He toured those remote areas where gaining support for a separate Muslim nation became his priority. There appeared no end to his spree of visits, speeches and lectures. Begum Liaqat in these circumstances had taken up the reins of management of the 'Gul-e-Ra'ana' household, her two small children, Ashraf and Akbar, and was also able to give time for party work. Even in the absence of Liaqat Ali, her home was agog with activities, throngs of visitors and their debates.

If we talk only of Ra'ana Begum's sacrifices, they were out of the ordinary. She epitomised a woman's inexhaustible love for her husband. Even with her background of a different religious allegiance, her role as a supporter of her husband's mission of creating a new nation gradually took shape, as the intensity of passion for his work increased to the point of crazy obsession. She was firmly committed to his dream. Any other woman in her place would have given up and accepted defeat or would have gone into depression.

Muhammad Ali Jinnah had gone through a shattering experience at his home which led to the death of his wife whom he loved so intensely. She was not a political person like him. Ra'ana Begum's mettle was quite different. Once determined to do a thing, she had the habit of going deep into the finer aspects of it. She had resolved to go into the subtle points which would bring to completion the creation of Pakistan. Ra'ana Begum had one advantage. Her very close and special friend Kay Miles used to keep close to her like a shadow, and was capable of not only reading her mind but knew very well the accomplishments and works of Liaqat, his needs and priorities. Once the Principal of Lucknow's Karamat Hussain College, Kay Miles was a pleasant personality, ever-smiling, a cordial woman by nature. Her presence in the close vicinity always filled the house with cheer and positivity. Whenever Ra'ana Begum along with Liaqat or even alone appeared too busy in her political work, Kay Miles proved a great help and perfectly reliable. Ra'ana Begum could rest assured of her assistance in looking after her children and her home without hesitation. This was not a small matter. When Liaqat and Ra'ana Begum flew to their new destination, Pakistan, Kay Miles accompanied them.

Remembering his mother, Ra'ana Begum's elder son Ashraf said:

> I do not recall if she ever got angry with me, whereas we were neither innocent nor sweet-tempered. The lessons in discipline and educational cooperation that we learned came from our dear Madame Billy (Kay Miles)'.

Ra'ana Begum or Irene was not in any sort of contact with her family. Her younger brother and sister had finished their education and were making satisfactory progress in life. Norman, who was her playmate and of almost similar age, having completed law had gone into legal services. In 1938 he married a girl from the family residing in Indore. His son, Jitendra got more and more thrilled as he came to know about his aunt's adventures and accomplishments. He was very proud of her and conserved everything related to her. At the time of the funeral of Ra'ana Begum, the only male member to be present from her father's side was Jitendra.

Famine, World War II and Transfer of Power

This was a time of frightful uncertainty. On one hand, the entire world was engulfed in the horrors of World War II, on the other, in British India, people were facing a situation of indecisiveness. Circumstances were converging to a point where anything could happen, anytime. In a way, the chain of events in Europe had the effect of slowing down the movement for freedom in India. In Britain, premiership went to Sir Winston Churchill after Arthur Neville Chamberlain. Those aware of the history of those days understand what contempt Churchill had for India's nationalist spirit. The Transfer of Power to Indians was not on his agenda either. He spared no chance of ridiculing popular, respected leaders like Mahatma Gandhi and the struggling Indian masses and wished to smash their movement. On the contrary, the Great War had allowed the Indians to exert double pressure on the British rulers to agree to their demands and intensify the agitation. There appeared differences though, on the question of what should be the character of the movement. In such a situation, marked by conflicting opinions, Mahatma Gandhi softened his stance on Civil Disobedience, seeing Britain's weakening position in the war. He decided that only a few select leaders would sit on protest demonstrations. However, despite this, the country saw a dramatic rise in protest marches and speeches, which is clear from the fact that in 1941 about 14,000 *satyagrahi*s were rounded up.

Japan's attack on Pearl Harbour in December 1941 ensured that the US would join the war in defence of its interests. While this development led to the strengthening of Britain's position, as it got a good ally, the fierceness of battles did not appear to slacken. By April 1942, the Japanese had made their way through Dutch East India (today's Indonesia), Singapore, Malay right up to Burma. The frightened British needed India's help. Taking into account the vulnerable position of Britain, Mahatma Gandhi took a practical step of postponing the *satyagraha*. However, he expressed a strong view against involving Indian people in the war because it went against the principles on which he had been waging his fight. A historic day in India's persistent struggle for freedom was 8 August 1942, for on that day Gandhi launched the nation-wide 'Quit India' movement. It roused the entire population of the country despite a few differences among the leaders, for in general awakened a great enthusiasm all over the length and breadth of the country. Contrary to this surging energy, the Muslim League kept itself away from the movement. It was Jinnah's opinion that if at this critical moment the British left India, their interests would receive a serious setback. He felt that Indian Muslims would be at the mercy of the Hindus. This prompted him to openly declare a boycott of the movement. This strategy proved effective, which is evident from the fact that soon the membership campaign of the League went up drastically.

While on one hand Congress leaders had been engaged in anti-war campaigns, on the other there were a large number of such elements who sided with the British in the hope of petty gains and favours like good jobs and money. At such a time another calamity struck the country. In 1943, Bengal experienced the worst famine in memory. Government mismanagement and poor handling of the crisis resulted in the death of millions; epidemic and paucity of medical help compounded the difficulties of common men and women. There prevailed chaos and utter disorder in society. In Bengal alone, more than three million people died of starvation. In 1940-42, the situation was gradually worsening; streets and roads were littered with dead and half-dead, abandoned to rot. They presented a pathetic and ugly sight of human misery and government's inhuman apathy. The famine and its wide publicity in newspapers and magazines, accompanied by heart-rending photographs, added to the already simmering displeasure against the British. In 1943, the tragedy had reached its worst pitch even though average rainfall was recorded above normal. It is said that this was a man-made famine, the result of the callous and inhuman policies of the British government, and not because of climate reasons. Even before 1943 natural calamities, diseases affecting crops and the fall of Burma combined to create conditions which badly affected food supplies to Bengal. Burma, which used to be a major exporter of rice, had then fallen into Japanese hands. Many experts believe that though these conditions created serious difficulties, it was not such an impossible condition as to completely cut off supply lines to Bengal or that proper arrangements could not be made. The major reason was the tendency to hoard food and grains and most of the deaths occurred because huge quantities of food were illegally hoarded, thus preventing it from reaching the common men who were starving. Prices soared high, much beyond common man's reach, and black marketeers ruled the roost. The government appeared to have lost control over the situation.

Subsequent investigations and researches brought to light the fact that during the war, it was the British Prime Minister's decision and tactical mistakes made by the War Council which were mainly responsible for exacerbating the pain and creating starvation conditions. It showed extraordinary insensitivity and absence of wisdom in handling such an enormous calamity. They were already given intelligence that excessive utilisation of India's resources and food material for war purposes might lead to a famine-like situation. But the stubborn British Prime Minister Churchill blatantly ignored the signs. Indiscriminate export to overseas British colonies from India continuously went on which finally resulted in this colossal tragedy. In 1942-43 the Chief Representative of the British administration, the then Viceroy requested the Prime Minister for immediate import of ten lakh tons of wheat. Churchill refused the request and ordered additional export of grain to some marked colonies from India. Churchill at the same time showed surprisingly crass insensitivity by making this savage remark, 'Indians are in the habit of breeding like rats...this famine is the result of that habit.'

He didn't stop there. On another occasion, instead of taking measures for better management of the crisis, he observed snidely, 'If the condition is so bad, why didn't the Mahatma (Gandhi) die?'

Churchill's India policy was so inhuman that not only were huge quantities of rice exported out of the country but the boats and other vessels along the Bengal coasts were seized so that it would not be convenient for local people to access food from across the borders. In this context, it would be relevant to remember that in 1873-74 the then Chief Administrator of Bihar, Richard Temple, not only took the surprising step of importing food but made efficient arrangements to reach it to the needy people and also initiated all kinds of welfare schemes. This was done with such superior vision and skill that not a single life was lost in Bihar. As a reward, he was severely criticised for making use of the British government's financial resources to save the lives of the famine-affected people.

In this grave situation, leaders of both Congress Party and Muslim League felt uncomfortable. A World War on one hand, and the great famine on the other. Added to this was the stark indifference of the British administration, which could not be ignored. Liaqat Ali Khan, addressing the Central Legislative Assembly, expressed his feelings in these words, 'Is it not a fact that because of this war millions have lost their lives in our country due to starvation? In this House, can anyone say that we have forgotten that there is a war going on and India comes under the direct and close impact of it?' This shrewd diplomatic statement put in the dock both the British rule and Congress leadership. If the process of events that had been going on for years can be summed up succinctly in a few words: World War II, Bengal famine, the growing social, political consciousness of the Indian people and the position of British power on the world map—all these factors precipitated the fall of the mighty British and paved the way for India's liberation. It is also true that this resulted in the Partition of the country, the pain of which seeped deep into the psyche of the population on both sides of the new borders and continued to gnaw their souls for generations.

It must have been in the concluding days of the year

1943 that the senior Congress leader Bhulabhai Desai, keeping within the provisions of the Indian Government Act 1935 met Liaqat Ali to discuss the formation of the united government of Congress and Muslim League. This formally came to be called the Liaqat-Desai Pact.

Newspaper reports of this meeting led to a lot of rumours and misunderstandings. These misunderstandings snowballed into such a controversy as to produce differences between Muhammad Ali Jinnah and Liaqat Ali Khan. The latter had already made it quite clear that this meeting was just a formal talk—the real, serious discussion could only be held between Mahatma Gandhi and Muhammad Ali Jinnah. However, the debate grew to such proportions that the British government promptly contacted Jinnah to clarify his position. Jinnah denied knowledge of and consent to any such agreement. Liaqat had to work hard to do damage control. Even today, whenever the Liaqat-Desai documents are mentioned, his moves are seen with a degree of suspicion. As usually happens, rumours spawned and proliferated with incredible speed—one of them making rounds of the country concerned Jinnah's health as he was reported to be on his deathbed. Liaqat dismissed such talk as a mere figment of imagination. The War saw the end of its originator, the die-hard racist, fascist and obstinate Adolf Hitler, but nobody knew when and how the scars left by this horrifying war would be erased. In the literal sense, it had broken the backbone of a power that boasted that the sun would never set on its vast empire. The War triggered an era of decolonisation the world over and weakened the military power of those who believed in imperialism. The best of the younger generation had laid their lives; the economy had been shattered beyond hope of recovery. Indians suffered alongside the British fighters and became target of worst assaults from the enemy. The finest cities of the world were reduced to rubble in reckless German bombings—re-building these cities posed a tough challenge to peacetime leaders. For this, it was necessary to create an atmosphere of peaceful cooperation among all the nations.

At this juncture, the British rulers were ready to take India's problem to a decisive stage. In the prevailing conditions, it became quite difficult for them to suppress the surging feelings of nationalism in India and finally to maintain their hold over it. For them, the priority was to put England back on its feet—all else came afterwards, which showed political pragmatism.

The government convened a meeting on 25 June 1945 to consider the form and structure of the Executive Council in India. Along with MA Jinnah, Liaqat Ali Khan also participated, but the Congress did not agree with the Muslim League's idea to include representation of all other communities. The meeting ended without a decision.

Sir Winston Churchill gave up the post of Prime Minister after World War II. His successor was Clement Atlee, who from the beginning favoured India's independence. In any case, the impact of holding overseas colonies had been far from wholesome—

they were beginning to prove negative assets. The best option was to vacate them. Lord Wavell declared general elections for constituting the Legislative Assembly as a first step towards granting self-rule to Indians. Around this time, another wave of popular anger arose due to the decision taken by the British government to initiate legal proceedings against three chief officers of Subhash Chandra Bose. It is also a fact that the Congress had not so far supported these officers. But now the party came forward to defend them which further intensified anti-British feelings in the country. Finally, the British rulers withdrew these cases, creating among the masses a feeling of gratitude for the party. The result was that Congress registered a resounding victory in non-Muslim constituencies, bagging 97 per cent of votes. They were in a position to form governments in eight states.

Similarly, the Muslim League showed their hold over reserved seats in provincial assemblies and captured all Muslim seats in the Legislative Assembly. Expectedly, it emerged as the pioneer and champion of Muslim sentiments which only promoted the two-nation idea and politics in India. Its claim that only the League truly represents Muslims was getting proved. Now Jinnah had a fine excuse for demanding an independent Muslim country. But despite these landslide successes, the Muslim League was able to form the government only in Sindh and Bengal. In Punjab and North-West Provinces, despite commanding a substantial Muslim population, the governments that came to be formed had Congress in the lead role, supported by Sikhs and the Union Party of India.

Congress had resolved to participate in the Constituent Assembly. After long discussions and debates, the Viceroy on 15 June 1946, invited fourteen Congress leaders to participate in the interim Government, with Jawaharlal Nehru as its chief. On behalf of the Muslim League, Jinnah and Liaqat Ali Khan were selected. Besides, other communities and religions were represented by their respective leaders. Jinnah authorized Liaqat Ali to conduct the discussion on Cabinet Mission.

Later on, Liaqat was made Finance Minister in the cabinet, responsible for drawing up the country's maiden budget. Maximum care was taken of the poor sections and all kinds of provisions were made to safeguard their interests. Those associated with the work confirm that he was assisted in crafting it by his wife Ra'ana Begum. Liaqat Ali Khan termed it as a 'Socialist Budget', but the industrial sector was quite dissatisfied. They accused him of imposing harsh taxes, targeting their interests and even charged him with an obvious bias against the Hindus. His budget proposed 25 per cent tax on a profit of Rs 1 lakh and doubled corporate tax. In this controversial budget, Liaqat Ali promised to take strong action against tax evaders by constituting a Commission to look into such cases. While the Socialist-minded elements in the Congress Party gave support to the budget, Sardar Patel felt that Liaqat Ali Khan was proceeding in a well-planned manner against such reputed Hindu entrepreneurs as Ghanshyam Das Birla, Jamana Lal Bajaj and Balchand. These industrialists were close to Congress and generously funded the Party. Birla had taken some leading industrialists to found the Indian Chamber of Commerce and Industries in 1927. He was a committed nationalist, a devotee of Gandhi and was always ready to make funds available for the Congress party's needs. Liaqat Ali's budget must have created a crippling effect on Muslim and Parsi businessmen, but as it happened, numerically Hindus surpassed them.

The Muslim League had acquired a decent and respectable representation now, but their demand was for a separate nation which they didn't have the means to obtain. Considering this, Jinnah made up his mind to directly address the issue without loss of time to exploit Muslim sentiments to the utmost, at the same time maintaining pressure on the British government. To highlight this demand, he called on people to observe 16 August 1946 as the Direct Action Day. Passion was building up when things turned violent, as in Calcutta the Chief Minister Hussain Shahid Suhrawardy's public speech proved provocative enough to ignite a communal conflagration. Waves of violence travelled from Noakhali in Bengal, Bihar, Garh Mukteshwar in UP to Rawalpindi. The riots affected large sections of the population which saw the death of 5,000 people and one lakh displaced. The situation went out of control to such an extent that while in one place it was suppressed, at another place it exploded anew. There appeared to be no solution to this murderous spree which continued to rage all over the country. It appears that it was one of the reasons for Congress to concede to the creation of Pakistan by splitting the country. Mahatma Gandhi was against Partition till the last moment of his life, so much against it that he declared that the country's Partition will be done only over his corpse. But men and women had turned into ferocious animals, killing and plundering in a frenzy. Suspicion and mistrust lurked in everyone's heart. No one was safe and happy.

Finally, towards the end of 1946, the ruling Labour Party of Britain officially authorised British rulers in India to leave the country. The British Parliament, after a long sitting and debate, eventually passed a resolution to this effect. Probably, they had no option. However, nothing tangible in the shape of a plan to Partition India had come about and there was as usual lack of co-ordination and confusion among the Congress, the Muslim League and the British rulers. One point on which the two large parties agreed was that India's 23 Viceroy Lord Wavell's role on the issue of Partition and related matters was not proper. All kinds of charges began to be levelled against him. Mahatma Gandhi, Jawaharlal Nehru, Muhammad Ali Jinnah and Liaqat Ali Khan severely criticised Lord Wavell's conduct. The British government did not want to get involved in any new controversy at a time when the mother country was making efforts to heal its wartime wounds. It was during his tenure that the Bengal famine of 1943 had occurred. It was also under his rule that the

Rajagopalachari formula of 1944 had been presented and in 1945 World War II ended with Japan's abject surrender. The country also saw under Lord Wavell the Direct Action Day, Cabinet Mission and formation of the Indian Government under Pandit Jawaharlal Nehru but the Viceroy's relations with people were always marked by some controversy or the other.

Clement Richard Atlee, giving serious thought to Lord Wavell's performance as the Viceroy found him unsuitable for the job. Atlee himself was not an exceptional leader. He was considered ineffective even in his public relations but he possessed a grave personality and a better image. People liked him for his impartiality, decision-making and scholarly habits. For these qualities, he was chosen as the Prime Minister, which set him apart from his competitors. After giving a good deal of thought to the question, he decided to send Lord Louis Mountbatten as the next Viceroy of India. He was one of the close relatives of King George, had a good image, enjoyed the reputation of an effective speaker and was efficient in public relations.

Towards Freedom

A descendant of the English Royal family, fourth Prince Louis of Battenberg, Louis Francis Albert Victor Nicholas, had visited India sometime at the age of 21 years. He must never have imagined in his dreams that he would one day be in a position of carrying the singular responsibility of decision-maker at a critical juncture of the Indian subcontinent's history. During World War II he was the Supreme Commander of South-Asian Command on the side of Allied forces. That gave him a fair knowledge of India and the surrounding areas.

When on 18 December 1946 the newly elected Prime Minister Clement Atlee invited Lord Mountbatten for the post of India's Viceroy, he was serving in England's Navy as Rear Admiral. The war was over. Being India's Viceroy meant being the administrator chief of 20 per cent of the world's population, next only to the Queen in wielding power. It was unthinkable for anyone to decline such an offer. But he found himself truly in a puzzling situation when Atlee invited him to take up the post. He arrived as the last Viceroy of India on 20 March 1947 and soon realised that he was in the middle of a mind-boggling set of circumstances. Delhi was caught up in the vortex of violent incidents, riding on a high tide of communal passion. The situation was nearly out of control. Not only Delhi but the entire country was rocked by fierce waves of bloodthirsty events. Distrust and mutual hatred pervaded the air. To bring Congress and the Muslim League to a sensible dialogue, to put popular emotion on a leash and to find a peaceful solution to the problem of partition presented hard challenges.

A peculiar situation existed in India at that time. The Labour Party in Britain had declared independence for India. In this country, the Interim coalition governments of Congress and Muslim League had proved to be utter failures. The country was getting swallowed up in the ugliest forms of violence. Jinnah harped on Pakistan and Congress wanted undivided India. Viceroy Lord Wavell was unable to bring both Congress and Muslim League to a compromise. Before him, Lord Linlithgow had tasted similar bitter failure in his efforts. To become Viceroy under these circumstances meant to risk one's clear image. Mountbatten knew it very well. His wife Edwina, his mother Princess Victoria and other well-wishers tried to convince him, but he was resolved now. It is said that it was his dream to become the Viceroy of India which he had long been cherishing. This is mentioned in his book, *Mountbatten and the Partition of India*. When he first visited India in 1921, he was dazzled by the pomp and luxury of the Viceroy's lifestyle which kindled in his heart a desire to enjoy the exalted position. But he wanted to come here on his own terms. Before consenting, he held long sessions with Atlee about officers and aides of his choice; a new aeroplane, and after returning to England restoration of his old post in the Navy. These were accepted without any hitch—it is said that Atlee agreed to every single demand. On 22 March 1947, he arrived in India with unprecedented powers. Lord Wavell was then in India; this was the first time that the outgoing and the incumbent were present at the same time. It was Mountbatten who had broken the protocol. It was through him that the fate of many leaders was to be written afresh.

Mountbatten was quite convinced before and after coming to India that no matter how highly educated Jinnah was, it was almost impossible to convince him. This opinion was voiced by him many a time on several occasions:

'Jinnah is an obstinate and stubborn person, and because of him India was fragmented.'

He had known Jawaharlal Nehru from earlier times; they had met in Malaysia in 1946. He also knew that if he was to be successful, Mahatma Gandhi should be taken along. Before bargaining with Gandhi, he must know all that about him of which Gandhi himself was not aware. Meetings between the two were fixed every Monday because it is said Gandhi used to observe silence on that day. Mountbatten felt that it was difficult to get him around to agreeing to Partition by mere arguments. Gandhi was quite a match to him: he would keep a small pack of old, used envelopes and would write his answers on the back of them. Mountbatten conserved these envelopes all his life.

India was facing the condition of a civil war, for Hindu-Muslim hostilities had reached the utmost limit and the public appeared divided along communal lines. It was clear to Mountbatten that a quick resolution of the problem was in the interest of all. Under a well-thought-out strategy, he restored the glitzy and glamorous Viceregal lifestyle. This dazzled the Indian leaders and his weight in discussion with them increased. On the other side, he gave the impression of a simple-hearted being. His common repertoire included unscheduled meetings with Nehru at his residence when he liked to have lunch or dinner with him, going for long walks with his wife with armed guards, and casually meeting common people. This had the expected impact and he certainly looked different from other Viceroys. Before embarking on his mission to India, Mountbatten wished to know from Atlee the definite period of his tenure in office. Atlee proposed summer of 1948, but Mountbatten wanted even the day and month fixed. So Atlee suggested

January 30, 1948, as the day when the Transfer of Power would begin. This was accepted.

In May 1947, Mountbatten who was also known as 'Dicky' went to Shimla where Nehru accompanied him. There Nehru was shown the draft which was to get approval of the British Parliament. Mountbatten wanted Nehru to have a good look at the plan and suggest amendments. When on 3 June 1947 the plan received approval of the British government, it came to be called the 'Mountbatten Plan'. He told Gandhiji that the Plan was structured the way he had wished it to be, so it would be better if it were called 'Gandhi Plan'.

Mountbatten made it clear that if the two major parties, Congress and Muslim League, did not reach an agreement over the issue of 'Transfer of Power' then it would be difficult to stop the partition of the states as well. He also put forward different alternatives which included the division of Bengal, Assam and Punjab. Telling Liaqat about the damage such a move entailed, he said,

'If we are the enemies of India, we shall have departed from the country in June 1948, but Indian masses have gone out of control these days and they will agree to the suicidal plan also.'

Then Liaqat Ali also admitted that the mentality of the masses had become like that, but it appeared that even some Congress leaders along with Jinnah did not wish to logically read popular feelings.

According to the Plan, the country would be divided

into two parts, both would be given dominion status. Bengal and Punjab would also be divided. Princely states would be given the choice of remaining free or merging with either of the two countries. Mountbatten did not stop there. He surprised everyone by declaring that the British would quit India on 15 August 1947. On the third point, he leaned towards India. Two weeks before independence, he addressed the princely rulers and Nawabs of the 'Chamber of Princes' and cautioned them. 'The native princely rulers will be the rudderless boats after the departure of the British, and if they do not choose to merge with India, only they will be responsible for the resultant anarchy.' He then said, 'You cannot run away from your closest neighbour India nor can the Queen of London guarantee your security. Better it would be if you stopped dreaming of existing independently and it would be in the interest of everyone to merge with the Indian Union'. The effect of this address was that by 15 August 1947 most of the princely rulers and Nawabs had put their signatures on the instrument of accession.

There was a reason why Lord Mountbatten chose 15 August. This was the day when Japan surrendered to the Allied forces. It must be remembered that before the US dropped an atomic bomb over the Japanese cities Hiroshima and Nagasaki, Lord Mountbatten had led his forces to a resounding victory over Japan in the battle for Burma. There was no other more significant date than 15 August where the Japanese capitulation and India's complete freedom coalesced. Mountbatten was, no doubt, the favoured officer of the former Prime Minister Winston Churchill, but the latter viewed Mountbatten's role in the partition of the country and liberating colonies from English dominance with great suspicion. That's why after his return to England in 1948, Churchill never talked to him. He was truly displeased with Mountbatten's role in the matter of independence of India and Pakistan. Mountbatten used to consider himself free to think and act, and now a person like Winston Churchill had no importance for him—he followed his own agenda.

At the time of his departure, Lord Wavell left certain questions for Mountbatten to tackle. One of them pertained to the furore which arose from Finance Minister Liaqat Ali Khan's budget presented before the interim government. It was Liaqat's duty to present facts regarding the Muslim League before the Viceroy, but their talk mainly focused on the stalemate his budget had created.

Liaqat Ali had met Lord Mountbatten twice before the latter held extensive discussions with Jinnah on two nations and two communities. In one such meeting, Liaqat had made it clear to Mountbatten that after going through the painful experiences of communal riots and the bitterness prevailing in the Interim government, it was impossible to think of one nation. He said, 'Instead of working with Congress, if we are given the barren desert of Sindh as a nation, we'd accept it.'

This was Jinnah's tactical policy which was being implemented through Liaqat Ali Khan, and Lord Mountbatten took no time in understanding this. The truth is that the chief demand of Jinnah had been partition. There was another aspect, and that was division of the Indian Army. Liaqat and Jinnah wanted even the army to be neatly partitioned! But Mountbatten showed a sense of practicality about it. He said that it was not possible to do this until June 1948. According to analysts, it would take at least five years for the Indian Army to form itself in the absence of British officers. But Jinnah was insisting on reducing this period to just one year.

On one hand, Lord Mountbatten was baffled, and on the other the Commander-in-Chief of Indian Army Sir Claude Auchinleck opposed such a move. He said that in the disturbing situation of the society the talk of dividing the country's army would result in a drop in the morale and work efficiency of the forces. The Viceroy tried to impress on Jinnah this delicate point, but the latter was in no mood to listen. Then it was felt that this question was best left to experts. While rounds of talks continued, the entire country including Delhi was going through an unabated rioting and spree of killings, suspicion and distrust rode the air and faith in each other's loyalty had fled.

The new Viceroy not only held discussions with Gandhi and Jinnah, but tried to include such diverse leaders as Jawaharlal Nehru, Liaqat Ali Khan, Sardar Vallabh Bhai Patel, Sikh leaders Master Tara Singh and Baldev Singh, and take them into confidence. Lord Mountbatten's wife Edwina also joined him in his work as time was short and considerable work remained to be done. She, like Begum Liaqat Ali Khan, used to take interest in women's health problems and their welfare. They, therefore, got along very well. Edwina won the confidence of Amrit Kaur, who was called the right hand of Mahatma Gandhi. She was also close to the leader of Dalits (socially depressed classes), Dr BR Ambedkar, firebrand women's leader Kamla Devi Chattopadhyay and the poet-politician Sarojini Naidu. She was in close contact with top women leaders of both Congress and Muslim League.

The tempest of violence continued to escalate rather than diminish. There appeared no solution to it but the partition of the country. The situation of desperation reached such a point that Pandit Nehru warned Mountbatten that if he did not have any work plan which was not passed quickly, he'd disengage himself from the issue. In the middle of May, Mountbatten sailed to England to work out a final draft. By the end of May, he returned and presented the plan regarding partition.

History records that on 3 June 1947, Mountbatten called a meeting of nationalist leaders Jawaharlal Nehru, Vallabhbhai Patel, JB Kripalani and from the Muslim League Muhammad Ali Jinnah, Liaqat Ali Khan and Abdul Rab Nishtar, and representative of the Sikhs Baldev Singh; within hours they had to announce the partition proposal. According to it, areas where Muslims were in majority were to go with Pakistan and India was to retain Hindu and Sikh majority areas. All members gave consent to it the next day.

Thereafter, Mountbatten fixed 15 August 1947 as the

day when power was to be transferred whereas, the British government had given 1 June 1948 as the deadline. On 18 July 1947, the British Parliament also endorsed it. It is also a fact that Mahatma Gandhi completely disagreed with any plan for partition while Nehru agreed to it to a great extent. In the prayer meeting held on 3 June, he mentioned that Pandit Nehru was the unproclaimed leader of the country but if the ruler forgets that in a democracy, the people should remind him what and where things go wrong. Next day, after the Mountbatten-Gandhi meeting the Viceroy wrote:

'Seeing the destruction of the dream of a United India, I feel as much pain as Gandhiji.'

But he also stated:

'The Partition plan was accepted after considering all other options. There could be a peaceful and quick transfer of power in no other way.'

It is not that Muhammad Ali Jinnah gave importance only to Liaqat Ali Khan—this is written by Mountbatten in his report:

'I have no idea who Jinnah's friends were but I know that his main friend was the Nawab of Bhopal. Only three days ago he told me that Jinnah wished to have his advice on Partition. The Nawab told him that it would be a mistake to retain the Governor-General and the British officers.'

After talking to Liaqat Ali Khan, it was clear that he also thought along these lines. Mountbatten also told Jinnah:

'Don't insist on becoming Governor-General,

because it is only a constitutional post and a Governor-General can only offer advice. You can rule Pakistan only as a Prime Minister in the true sense.'

To this Jinnah replied:

'Whatever I say, others will have to listen.'

It then became clear that he was not willing to accept anything below the position of Governor-General. Finally, Lord Mountbatten remarked:

'You'll have to pay a price for it, do you know that?'

Jinnah replied:

'Pakistan will be losing property worth a few crores.'

Mountbatten said:

'Along with this, you'll be losing Pakistan's future too.'

This did not affect Jinnah. Mountbatten had taken charge as the Chairman of the Pakistan Council, with MA Jinnah and Liaqat Ali Khan as Muslim League representatives. Abdul Rab Nishtar was the optional member. The Congress was represented by Rajendra Prasad and Sardar Vallabhbhai Patel, while their optional member was C Rajgopalachari. The process of partitioning India was almost nearing completion. Britain had offered the subcontinent's 567 princely states the choice to merge with either of the two countries, which created some problems. Sardar Patel took a firm stand on the issue while Mountbatten sided with VP Menon.

As per the resolution, British lawyer Sir Cyril Radcliffe was nominated the Chairman of the Indian Boundary Committee which was to draw a line of 4,50,000 km over the land inhabited by millions of people and split it into two countries. He had finished his work on 13 August, but the 'Radcliffe Line' was disclosed purposely on 17 August to avert any untoward happenings on the independence day of both the countries. A writer notes:

> '1947 was the year of the infernal conflagration which in its red heat was melting the moulds of human habitations to create boundaries of the two "nations". Radcliffe Line was nothing but a macabre, raw graveyard of the molten, gutted corpses, dwellings and, more significantly, co-operation such as was built over thousands of years between the communities in which were being thrown those who had not yet died but were still alive in their senses and feelings.'

Radcliffe's task was enormous, leaving much probability for human error and controversies. Some errors were claimed to have been intentionally left, some were the result of diplomatic problems. Though the general impression is that the British government was not in favour of the breakup of the country, this undoubtedly, was their handiwork. The two communities and two-nation theory was thus taking solid form. It was a surprising decision—it gave birth to two mutually uncomfortable countries whose people always looked at each other with undiminished suspicion and distrust. Only the future could reveal how the decision was going to be justified, but all knew that this was not in the interest of the two communities. This is the boundary where the Urdu writer Sa'adat Hassan Manto's famous character in his story, 'Toba Tek Singh' dies after getting entangled in the strange conflict. His dead body lies on the line, half this side and half that side. It is said that the story is the finest portrayal of man's interests, impetuosity and fine-tuned sensibilities.

In these hard times, Liaqat Ali Khan and his Begum Ra'ana were pursuing their goal with all honesty, perseverance and dedication. This was the goal with which they had identified their life at every step of its progress and seen its fulfilment. Despite many hurdles and impediments, they had stuck to it; when one felt fatigued, the other would lend a supportive hand. This journey gave them the relish and pleasure of working together. They had seen Ruttie Jinnah withering away into death's dark chamber despite Jinnah's honest love and attachment. They had walked through life's highs and lows that affected them as much as others. Now they were waiting for this moment which was so close to their hearts. But they were as much pained by the communal riots as any honest person would be. All around them, the most savage and brutal massacres were taking place in which women and children were the most vulnerable targets. Such brutality they couldn't have imagined even in their dreams. The orgy of violence didn't show signs of stopping. These scenes shook Ra'ana Begum to the core; she was emotionally moved. In these tragic moments, Ra'ana Begum revived her women's organisation which had deep roots in North India. She resolved to help the affected women and children. The surprising thing about it was that she knew that this country was no longer hers and she'd have to leave it for her new country. But despite this, she put her heart into providing succour to women in trouble and the idea of detaching herself from the people of this country never entered her mind. She continued to do her work, keeping up a good supply of food, clothes and medicines.

Jinnah was elected the Convener of the Constituent Assembly on his arrival in Karachi on 7 April 1947. A great banquet was organised at his official residence on the night of 13 August. Mountbatten was present with his wife Edwina. In keeping with the protocol, Ra'ana Begum and Jinnah sat in the middle. Both the elite ladies had a dig at Mountbatten for consulting an astronomer in the matter of choosing midnight to grant freedom to the two countries. Pakistan in this manner came into existence on 14 August 1947, while India became free on 15 August. Jinnah had made great preparations for the occasion. He had already sold his palatial residence at Aurangzeb Road to industrialist Ramkrishna Dalmia. On the other hand, Liaqat donated his close-to-heart 'Gul-e-Ra'ana' house to the Pakistan High Commission which is still being used as the official residence of the High Commissioner. Though Liaqat Ali Khan and Ra'ana Begum had the delight of seeing their dream of a Muslim majority country taking shape before their eyes, the pain of leaving India overwhelmed all other feelings. It was heart-rending, more so because they were born here, had been nourished and nurtured and breathed the free air of this land. They made it clear that they would take only their personal belongings with them and the rest of the goods would be left behind for the use of new occupants. Besides Liaqat's large collection of lighters, Ra'ana Begum wished to take along the carpet which was gifted to her by her mother. 'This is my mother's gift—I can't leave it here', she told Liaqat.

Begum Ra'ana prepared herself to bid *adieu* to India. She was born here. Its air had nourished her heart and mind. Her parent's families, vibrant and prospering, were still here. She was leaving it all behind forever. A nation was being born before her eyes. As the dates of the two countries' independence approached, the atmosphere grew tenser with the anticipation of greater violence. Murderous attacks on children, youth and women occurred on every street. Those who had never stepped out of their drawing rooms were dragged out and done to death for no fault of theirs. It was a frenzy of passion and an orgy of savagery; no street, no colony, no market place was exempt from this scene of inhuman behaviour. This was happening when there was a general consent about creating two nations and the steps couldn't be retracted. A pall of grief, bereavement and anguish hung just before the hour of independence. People were wary and scared. In Karachi, it was a common sight to see hordes of people running from one place to another, fleeing their flaming houses under a hail of bullets. Those families which had never stepped out of home were forced to scamper barefoot, distraught and unable to understand which way to go, for everywhere there were blood-stained hands ready to throttle them. The city was celebrating the country's Partition and the birth of Pakistan. India's Viceroy Lord Mountbatten and his wife Lady Edwina had arrived for the oath-taking ceremony of Pakistan's new Governor-General, Muhammad Ali Jinnah and proclaiming the end of the British Empire. Strikingly, there was neither Jinnah nor the Prime Ministerial candidate Liaqat Ali Khan to receive the last Viceroy. On behalf of the Pakistan government, Governor of Sindh province Ghulam Hussain Hidayatullah was sent to welcome him. The Muslim League people suffered from the peculiar delusion that by ignoring protocol and neglecting to attend the chief guests, the masses would hold the League in greater awe! In this connection, one more incident can be mentioned. Jinnah insisted that he be given a chair higher than that given to Lord Mountbatten, because he was Pakistan's Governor-General and Chairman of the Constituent Assembly and so made an issue of it: The British government handled this issue tactfully, arguing that Jinnah will officially become Governor-General only after India's Viceroy ceremonially swears him in. Till then all rights and authority will remain with the Viceroy. Besides, it was also clarified that even when Jinnah becomes Governor-General, his position will continue to be below that of the Viceroy.

No sooner had this matter of protocol and official

status been resolved than another question arose. A rumour was making the rounds that the Sikhs of Punjab were extremely unhappy and there was a conspiracy to kill Jinnah by throwing a bomb in the Assembly House while he was entering. When Mountbatten arrived, he was asked what he would like to suggest in the light of this revelation. He replied that it was not his decision—it has to be decided by Jinnah and his party, but when he realised that Jinnah himself put the responsibility of decision making on him, then Mountbatten replied:

'If anyone has hatched such a plot to blow up Jinnah then the possibility is that when I am with him such an assault will not be made because then two Governor-Generals will be simultaneously blown to pieces, one of India, another of Pakistan. Therefore, I have no problem going in such a procession.'

That meant that Mountbatten was not in favour of cancelling the programme. After this statement, all necessary arrangements were made for a high-security procession. After the function, when Jinnah and Mountbatten reached the Governor House safely, Jinnah, taking a deep sigh of relief, said, 'Thank God, I saved you!'

Mountbatten replied, 'Thank God, I too saved you!'

Before this, when on 2 June Lord Mountbatten convened a meeting of Indian statesmen at the North Court to place before them the plan of Partition, he told Indian leaders to acquaint him with their answers by midnight. When Jinnah left the place, Mountbatten noticed that he had during the meeting drawn some squiggly figures on a sheet of paper. They resembled tennis rackets, floating balloons, rockets, etc and inscribed under it the words 'Governor-General'. Anyone could guess by these doodles what was going through his mind. Qaid-e-Azam was thinking about the title for his future post. Tilak Deveshar, who once served as an officer in R&AW, the intelligence agency of India, claims somewhere:

'Lord Mountbatten had tried to get Jinnah in 1947, just one month before Independence, to agree to become joint Governor-General of India and Pakistan.'

Mountbatten argued that if Jinnah became Governor-General only of Pakistan, his functioning would be quite restricted. Jinnah remarked:

'Please don't bother about that. My Prime Minister will do what I tell him. I shall advise him and he will act on it.'

This is recorded in other places too.

Pakistan's President, Iskandar Mirza, who was also the Defence Secretary, said to Jinnah, 'We must take care of the Muslim League that has given us Pakistan.'

Jinnah promptly replied, 'Who says Muslim League gave us Pakistan? It is I who has put it on its feet with the help of my stenographer.'

The speech which he delivered on 11 August 1947 in the Constituent Assembly contained the old contradictions about Hindu-Muslim unity.

'We must assure the minorities in this country by our words, ideas and work of their being perfectly safe as long as they perform their duties as the nation's loyal citizens. They need not fear anything. We are inaugurating that era when there will be no segregation and differentiation and the two communities will be treated as equal. This fundamental principle of all citizens being equal forms the foundation of this country.'

Lord Mountbatten read out the message of King George the Sixth to the Constitution Committee and conveyed his greetings and best wishes for the new country. On 14 August, the coming into being of Pakistan was formally proclaimed. In his address to the nation, Jinnah congratulated millions of Muslims for their success in reaching their goal. He also gave assurance that people of all faiths will be allowed to live peacefully and a policy of peaceful relations with other countries will also be pursued.

In such circumstances was born Pakistan. It attained its freedom from Britain on one hand, and from India on the other. After almost 200 years, the Union Jack was lowered and Pakistan's flag was hoisted. In India, the Constituent Assembly was convened on 14 August and at midnight the country became free. Addressing the Assembly, Pandit Jawaharlal Nehru said:

> Long years ago, we made a tryst with destiny, and now the time comes when we shall redeem our pledge, not wholly or in full measure, but very substantially. At the stroke of the midnight hour, when the world sleeps, India will awaken to life and freedom. A moment comes, which comes but

rarely in history when we step out from the old to the new—when an age ends, and when the soul of the nation, long suppressed, finds utterance. At this solemn moment, we should take the pledge of dedication to the services of India, and her people, and to the still large cause of history.

Flight to Fame

When Liaqat Ali Khan, Ra'ana Begum, their sons Ashraf and Akbar landed at Karachi airport in two government planes, they felt a strange thrill. There was a sort of tentativeness, a little scepticism, but at the same time, Liaqat and Ra'ana Begum were brimming with excitement to put the newly created country on the path of self-reliance. They were aware of the enormous challenges confronted by them which could be handled only by the power of logic. Liaqat and Ra'ana Begum had been preparing themselves for the responsibility since long. They had been dreaming for years, and that dream had been realised. Credit goes to Liaqat and Ra'ana Begum for transforming the dream into reality, getting Jinnah to agree to return to India, making him powerful and consolidating the Muslim League identity, and changing his despair into hope. Putting aside their honeymoon sentiments, this newly married couple persuaded Jinnah to return to India and revive the Muslim League.

It is not for nothing that Jinnah considered Liaqat his right hand man. He knew that if there was anyone who could be called a trustworthy co-traveller of his political odyssey and confidant, it was Liaqat Ali Khan. There was a striking similarity in their thinking and opinions on almost every topic of significance. That is the reason the duo could play such a long innings together. Liaqat also found in his wife such a companion as he could hardly have imagined. At the time of their marriage in 1933, Liaqat had been nominated as the General Secretary of the Muslim League, no doubt, but there were no funds even for stationery and typing. In such difficult times, Ra'ana Begum came forward, learnt typing herself and with utmost sincerity, got down to replying to every letter that was received. She used to publicise the Party agenda, type the minutes and keep herself busy attending meetings meant for women's awakening.

With the separation of India and Pakistan amidst bloody violence and communal hatred, a new history was being written with names of the new protagonists, Liaqat Ali Khan and Ra'ana Begum, as the prime architects of this new country. It would not be an exaggeration to claim that Liaqat cherished a mega dream, to have freedom for the Muslim population of the sub-continent to enjoy cultural, political and social participation and get full justice which was possible only by creating a new nation.

At the command and desire of his mentor, Muhammad Ali Jinnah, Liaqat Ali Khan was sworn in as Pakistan's first Prime Minister on 15 August 1947. The country was still witnessing brutal assaults on its population and violence was far from over. Liaqat kept with himself the Foreign Ministry, Commonwealth Affairs and Defence Ministry. This naturally raised Ra'ana Begum's prestige and status. Jehanara Shahnawaz was the most active member of her women's empowerment organisation—she was also very active in the Muslim League. In 1918, she had formed the All India Muslim Women's Conference and adopted a resolution against the traditional practice of polygamy. She was elected as the member of Punjab State Legislative Assembly in 1937 and was nominated as Parliamentary Secretary in Education and Health Departments. During the Quit India movement in 1942, she became a member of the National Security Council. At that time, Muslim League had ordered all its members to resign from this Council, only she refused to do, and as a consequence had to face expulsion from the Muslim League. But four years later, she was taken back in the League and the same year selected as a member of the Central Constituent Assembly.

Begum Jehanara was not only close to Begum Ra'ana but like her was an avid activist for women's advancement. How she declined the offer of the post of Deputy Minister in the Pakistan government is recounted by her in her book. The book also made it evident that Begum Ra'ana used to play an important role in Liaqat's official decisions. She says that once she received a call from the Prime Minister's residence—when she went there, Begum Ra'ana met her. She requested Jehanara to accept the offer of Deputy Ministership. Once again declining it, Begum Jehanara reminded her that in the past she had worked as Parliamentary Secretary in undivided India, and after so many years it would be below her dignity to work on a lesser post. Her supporters would be greatly disappointed at this. She says that after this, Begum Ra'ana made an offer of appointing her as Ambassador to the Soviet Union. By then, Liaqat Ali Khan had also joined their discussion. Though turning down this offer, Jehanara observed that she was committed to all the Pakistani women who led a life of want, misery and are denied justice. It would not be possible for her to stay outside the country where she could not make any substantial contribution to allaying their pain. Since Ra'ana Begum and Liaqat Ali had been working together in perfect unison and shared one another's trust and dependability, they began to dedicate themselves to Pakistan's development. They had many visions and time was short for realising them. She, therefore, made utmost use of every available moment. For the time being, her priority was to create confidence and bring the disturbing social scenario under control. She had also to make adequate arrangements for the exodus of refugees crossing over the boundaries into Pakistan.

It may be considered a happy coincidence that the former Principal of Karamat College of Lucknow, Billy or

Kay Miles, went to Pakistan at the suggestion of Ra'ana Begum. She was a unique woman who was filled with great energy and restless passion for work. She was one of the most trusted friends of Ra'ana Begum. Before independence, she worked alongside Ra'ana Begum in organising Muslim women's rallies, managing them and in several related matters helping her constantly. Ra'ana Begum knew the importance of Billy and realised that without her she wouldn't find enough courage to face the tasks. Ra'ana Begum participated in the conference of Commonwealth national chiefs in London. The Soviet government invited her as the chief guest—Liaqat was in a dilemma and finally didn't go. President Harry S. Truman sent on 10 December 1949 a senior officer to Pakistan with an invitation for the Prime Minister to visit America in May 1950. This was accepted. The same year, he was elected National President of the Muslim League. When Ra'ana Begum as the first lady of Pakistan and wife of Liaqat Ali went to the US, she was seen as strongly representing her husband's views. Talking on the topic of 'Pakistan and the Modern World' at Kansas University, Liaqat said:

> 'We are living in that segment of time when the world's landscape is expanding. In a way, this is an age of the discovery of new nations. Four hundred years before, the European travellers discovered that sub-continent where we live today. They had found your land too. Because of your interest in the events of world history you are passing through a period where you can show your capabilities in

extending these voyages of discovery.

If I'm asked, the discovery of Asia is not yet complete. In truth, it has only begun. I'm sure that I can trust myself to strengthen those links in the chains binding the fates of your and my people which I know best and are dear to me.

Pakistan is a new country, or to be precise, a new democratic country. Three years of its birth as a democratic country are not yet completed. There was a time when the forces of democracy, human rights and freedom which are now well-entrenched were in their infancy, and the memories of your fight for those values were fresh. If you exercise your imagination for a while, you'd surely be able to understand that Pakistan's early history and the first three years of its freedom are merely a repetition of that history. A few years ago, Pakistan conjured only a passion and a concept. Britain ruled over that sub-continent where today Pakistan and India are situated; where 100 million Muslims have been living since centuries and made this land their home. Side by side, 300 million other people have also been living with them, among whom Hindus besides others had arrived far back in time and became the majority. As the moment of freedom for these 400 million people came closer, it came to be realised that 100 million Muslims would have to live perpetually all their lives under 300 million majority Hindus. After long experience gained over the ages, it was clear that freedom from Britain would mean just a change of masters; the form of slavery would remain unchanged. As has been commonly made out, this is not merely because of religious differences. It is not as easy to understand as to get an idea of the monotheism of Muslims and polytheism of Hinduism. Nor is it because the Muslims believe in the Prophet born in Arab, or the Christians believe in the Old Testament alone, and the Hindus do no such thing.

The difference is much wider and deeper which makes it evident that even the ordinary things of their day-to-day living are mutually incompatible. Hindus believe in a caste system according to which the higher caste considers it a sin even to sit and eat with those belonging to the lower castes or even to touch them; where the Muslims have always believed in equality of all to the extent they do not allow any one religion's superiority over others. They consider any Maulana or priest an obstacle to the connection that can exist between a devotee and Allah. They are, therefore, superfluous. From an economic point of view also the two communities are quite different.

There was good news for Ra'ana Begum. It became a matter of great pleasure for her to find that her younger brother George had decided to convert himself to Islam and live in Pakistan. He was re-named Jamil Parvez. Her other two brothers Henry and Arthur also promised to visit Pakistan from time to time. Begum Ra'ana herself visited India thrice. Separation of India and Pakistan into two countries was not an ordinary matter. This period of four years was full of challenges. Much had changed during this period. The great dreams had paled—a few of them had turned into nightmares. After India's Partition and the formation of two nations, Lord Mountbatten was least interested in staying back in India. He believed that after the transfer of power there was no attraction in filling the post of Governor-General after working as Viceroy. He also felt that this idea was destined to fail, which indeed it did. But it would not be proper to say that this was started by Mountbatten.

He told his friends that his wife Edwina did not want to stay here for long. But Muhammad Ali Jinnah put pressure on him not to go so soon for he feared that if he left, India would destroy Pakistan. It would not give financial assistance, but on the contrary, would deprive them of the weapons which they were obliged to supply under a pact. In short, it would not give them anything. He wanted the British government to see that they got their due. To this Lord Mountbatten put a counter-question, what does he expect from them in this regard? Jinnah replied that there ought to be two Governor Generals. Mountbatten remarked,

'That means that in a way the post of Viceroy should continue.'

Jinnah clarified:

'It'd be very difficult to continue the post of Viceroy but I'd always want to acknowledge you as Governor-General.'

Mountbatten put a question,

'Don't you think that by doing so there would arise an unnecessary controversy between the heads of the two nations?'

He then added, 'If there is a serious issue, I'm ready to continue as Pakistan's Governor-General till such a period as that issue is resolved. You can have the post of the Prime Minister. India's Prime Minister will be Nehru and the post of Governor-General will be only constitutional.'

But the question was not resolved, and there was no reference to this complication ever again.

It was not that Ra'ana Begum was alone in working for women's welfare and consciousness-raising with the spirit of a committed crusader. Muhammad Ali Jinnah's sister Fatima Jinnah was also with her and was always available for solving many a problem of Pakistani women. In bringing relief to the people and rehabilitating them, Fatima used to be at the forefront. In an interview given to *Dawn* on 25 August 1947, she talked about her tactical work:

> In creating Pakistan, women played a significant role in society...Women can play a greater role in society when they pay attention to getting educated. There would be launched an extensive educational campaign to uproot the ideas that

keep women uneducated and provide them with education. This will be a great step in creating an enlightened mother and her children the responsible citizens.'

Fatima tried to establish all kinds of educational institutions for women. When the British rulers were winding up their establishments in South Asia, there were only two medical colleges for women, both of them in India. In West Pakistan, there were a total of 118 women doctors and three in East Pakistan. The ratio of nurses was still more deplorable. It is said that only Hindus were admitted in Balakram Medical College and the medical college of Lahore affiliated with it. This situation, however, changed afterwards. The way Fatima Jinnah and Ra'ana Begum worked together for female education and made the government direct its resources for the purpose is a memorable effort. When in October 1948 a women's medical college began to function, it was named Fatima Jinnah Medical College. Fatima herself became its patron. At that time this was the only medical college administered by Muslims exclusively for women.

Edwina Mountbatten expressed a desire to personally visit the refugee camps of both the countries situated on the border and provide help. First, she went to the Pakistani Punjab and again in October, but by then the relations had reached such a pitch of tension that neither Fatima Jinnah came to welcome Edwina nor any woman came forward to greet her. It is said that when Edwina suggested that Fatima go across the border to India's refugee camps to offer help so that the tension between the two countries might be lessened, she squarely refused. Matters worsened to such an extent that Edwina's tour on 18 October was proposed to be postponed, which the then Governor of Punjab Francis Modi described as not safe for Edwina. But when without paying attention to their cautionary words she travelled to the camps, entry was refused to her because of the Kashmir dispute. However, despite these displays of stubborn attitude, some women thought these measures unwarranted.

If we compare Ra'ana Begum's work for the welfare of women with that of Fatima Jinnah, we'd be able to see that her range was greater and her work covered a wider area. The fact is that she had a rich experience of social work before 1947 in Indian society in which the main thrust was to awaken a general awareness in women and get them educated to make them self-reliant. It was an urgent call of the time to women and children to help one another in this crucial period. In the beginning, such camps were set up only in Lahore. In West Bengal alone there was an influx of 70,000 refugees. The 1947 Partition had created conditions where relief and acts of help were urgently required to put the bereaved population back on their feet and restore normalcy in their lives. That would enable them to take their own decisions. Ra'ana Begum mobilised like-minded women and launched a campaign for women's advancement. She had no problem sitting with low-class people and working with them. While she spent long hours with refugee women and children, she stayed at the forefront in her agitation for empowering women of the weaker sections. In her passion for social work, all had equal status, no one received a personal favour from her nor did she express any indifference for any unknown person. She, it is said, poured all her energy into building confidence in those weakened by social circumstances and needing to prove themselves. It was important for their survival.

Kay Miles, a close friend of Ra'ana Begum, has written in detail in her memoirs about that harrowing period. Among the basic duties to be performed in refugee camps was arranging for tents, food, clothes and medicine. It was also necessary to see that there occurred no scarcity of medicines for preventing the spread of deadly cholera and typhoid. Some of the medical centres were either understaffed or had more than the necessary number of workers. In such conditions, it had to be decided where the number of workers was to be reduced and where increased. This presented a peculiar challenge. People didn't easily come forward for service, especially in the profession of nursing, as these jobs were considered *infra dig*. Girls of Muslim families were ready to live a life of want and poverty but could not muster sufficient courage to enter the medical profession. Under these conditions, it was highly commendable that Ra'ana Begum managed to persuade Muslim girls to accept this opportunity to be of service to the suffering masses and earn in return profound blessings of all.

The result of all these efforts was that within the next two years, the nursing profession came to be looked upon as a respectable sector for women to seek employment. Ra'ana Begum provided them with much-needed motivation. It also opened a great opportunity of employment for Muslim women. Ra'ana Begum played a significant role in providing proper guidance to girls. She established the first Pakistan Nurse Foundation. Many nurses from this organisation joined the Army Medical Corps and made Pakistan proud of their great sacrifices.

Success came to her in whatever work she took up selflessly in a spirit of dedication. Not that she didn't face opposition; in fact, in the orthodox society of Pakistan it was inevitable that *maulvis* and religious fanatics raised voices of protest against Ra'ana Begum for showing Muslim women the 'wrong' path. Some newspapers also began writing against her ideas and campaigns. The couple soon found themselves standing at the crossroads where they saw the country of their dreams take shape in reality but time had begun putting those dreams to the acid test. Liaqat Ali Khan stood firmly by his wife. When circumstances turned too hostile, he openly came in support of her plans. In a public meeting, he said:

> Some people have serious complaints against my wife. A handful of people wonder where she is taking Pakistan. Is she trying to turn Pakistani women into 'dancing girls' by training them in the art of dance? No! She is inspiring them to go to the refugee camps to learn lessons in the service of

humanity. Is my wife motivating other women to visit gambling dens? No! She is motivating them to take up the nursing duties in hospitals which today's Pakistan urgently needs. Is it bad work?

Unmindful of the rising cacophony of criticism, Ra'ana Begum stuck to her mission of empowering women. She set up two institutions: Pakistan Women's National Guard and Pakistan Women's Naval Reserve. Though these also faced the usual protests, Ra'ana Begum ignored them. She became the director of these organisations, aposition equal to the rank of Brigadier. In the first Institute, a total of 2,400 volunteers were admitted and asked to go to different parts of the country. The aim of training these women was to prepare them to assist the armed forces. This was based on Ra'ana Begum's clear understanding that for the development, defence and prosperity of the country, capabilities of women should be as seriously utilised as is done concerning men. If Pakistan's four crore women were asked to sit at home, then the country could never be called a developing nation. The main thrust of the mission was to train young girls in defence tactics and perfect their physical skills. Their talents and achievements were demonstrated during various parade shows. Simultaneously, they were also trained in nursing services and first aid. Besides, instructions in typing and army signal system were also provided. Despite the conservative character of society which insisted on girls staying at home, it was surprising to see large numbers of enthusiastic young women come out of their homes to make their lives purposeful. The whole work, however, came to a standstill when Ra'ana Begum was sent to the Netherlands as Pakistan's Ambassador. The two institutes kept working for the next six years and proved the value of their existence in helping the armed forces which was possible only because of Ra'ana Begum's personal qualities.

Few people knew then that Jinnah whom people generally used to call 'Iron Man' was secretly very ill, even before World War II. His most reliable doctor had found in the medical reports that his lungs had such spots in them which might prove fatal and aggravate his tuberculosis. Medical science in those days had not developed so much that this simple ailment could easily be treated to save an important personality. Perhaps Lord Mountbatten knew about it. That is why he advanced the date of granting independence from February 1948 to August 1947. It is said that he knew that Jinnah was not destined to live long. If Gandhi, Nehru and Patel had known about his health, then, perhaps, they'd also have changed their policy and asked for more time for Partition because apart from Jinnah there was no other leader in the Muslim League who could not have been convinced to stop this act. The truth of the matter is that the process of creating the Pakistan Movement depended upon Jinnah. Liaqat Ali and the rest of the Muslim League leaders did not possess such a commanding influence over their followers that they could easily sway their opinion and get their support. Amid such hectic, bustling developments, March 1948 appeared to have arrived too soon. Jinnah was 72 and his health had deteriorated. He had experienced the most momentous day of his life and had got the position he wanted. His last days were spent in great pain. When on 11 September 1948, Jinnah was flown from Quetta to Karachi in a Viking plane, the weight of this life-long crusader for Pakistan had reduced to 40 kg. When an ambulance left for the Governor General's residence from Karachi's Mauripur airport, the van is reported to have run out of fuel midway. This was a painful situation. No one came out to receive the man who was the creator of Pakistan and on whom the country conferred the title of Qaid-e-Azam. With him at this crucial moment was his military secretary only. At that time Liaqat Ali Khan was the Prime Minister; his relations with Jinnah were not very good. Fatima Jinnah herself refers to this in her memoirs.

It took one hour for the military secretary to arrange for another ambulance. Till then, Jinnah lay in closed suffocating air inside the vehicle. His pulse was progressively getting feeble. At twenty minutes past ten that night, Jinnah was declared dead. His body was wrapped in a plain shroud and buried in Karachi.

To Liaqat Ali Khan and his wife Ra'ana Begum, who were struggling to create their place in Pakistan, which was itself in its infancy, Jinnah's demise was a big setback. In 1948, the Pakistan cabinet was reconstituted; soon afterwards Liaqat Ali faced a controversy over religious minorities in 1949-50.

Pakistan had come into being when the tug of war between the two superpowers, the US and the Soviet Union had reached its peak. Many questions confronted Liaqat Ali. First, he must chalk out the course of his country's development; second, he must have a balanced relationship with both the superpowers. Socialists in West Pakistan and Communists in the East were putting hurdles in his way in their characteristic manner. Faiz Ahmed Faiz, the Socialist leader in West Pakistan, was a popular leader because of which the appeal of the Muslim League and the government was increasing. In the East, Pakistan Communists had begun to erode the base of Muslim League. Great dissatisfaction was growing within the party. A particular faction influenced by the nationalist-socialist ideas and religious ideologies had become a persistent headache for the government. When in 1949, Joseph Stalin of the Soviet Union invited Liaqat Ali Khan on an official visit and the Pakistan PM did not reciprocate, the Soviet Union began to create many problems for him. The reality was that Liaqat was a supporter of the non-aligned foreign policy. But he did not understand that by rejecting the Soviet offer and accepting the US invitation, he had already destroyed his scheme. The Communist bloc thought that he was being dictated to the US in pursuing his policies, though he made it clear during his visit to America that he was for a policy of neutrality and would be consolidating it in future. It was also clarified that Liaqat's inability to go to the Soviet Union was mainly due to some sort of

Soviet dilemma and some contradictory forces in their internal policy.

Meanwhile, Liaqat got whatever help he demanded from America. The US always stood by Pakistan in terms of providing economic and moral strength. But things went awry when during the Korean War, the US asked for two combat units to be sent to the war. Liaqat put the condition that if the US promised to support Pakistan on Kashmir and Baluchi issues, he was ready to send his soldiers. For the US, this amounted to an insult—it declined to comply. Liaqat's refusal cleared the way to move in the direction of non-alignment. Commenting bitterly on American policy, the Pakistan PM said, 'Without your assistance, Pakistan has been able to occupy half of Kashmir, and now it is going to capture the rest of it too.'

On the other hand, Russia and China also showed courage to offer a straightforward reply, 'Pakistan has no time to wait; it will surely find friends when it needs them.'

In June-July 1951, US-Pakistan relations plummeted even further to a new low when during his US visit, Jawaharlal Nehru caused the US government to put pressure on Pakistan to order its troops to pull out of Kashmir. Several serious questions were confronting the governments of the two countries; for India, Kashmir was a prime issue. Liaqat made all efforts to get the Indian Prime Minister to come to the table and resolve the matter. At one stage it appeared that a solution was at hand when Pandit Nehru took the issue to the United Nations. But the matter couldn't be resolved as long as Liaqat and Nehru lived. It also soon became clear that Liaqat and Jinnah had serious differences over this problem.

Prime Minister Liaqat Ali Khan was a keen supporter of scientific and technical education in Pakistan, for which he began to initiate several steps. He believed that the country should be self-reliant and with this view he invited Rafi Mohammad Chowdhary, the eminent physicist. Similarly, not only was Salimuzzama summoned and given Pakistani citizenship but proclaimed to be the country's first Scientific Adviser to the national government. A significant measure in this series of planned steps was setting up of Sindh University for boosting higher education in that region. Restructuring science figured prominently in his rule for which he did not hesitate to invite those Indian engineers and scientists who could help the country formulate its policies and plans for future growth.

Suddenly Gone

'Begum, today is going to be a memorable day in Pakistan's history. Today I am going to make an important announcement.'

Pakistan's Prime Minister Liaqat Ali Khan jubilantly shared with his wife his feelings. In a few minutes, he was to leave for a public meeting he was scheduled to address.

'Oh, good! That's good news. Tell me something more about it.'

Her curiosity was mounting.

'No, not now! You're also one of those eight crore people—when they know, you'll also come to know,' Liaqat said to her. Begum Ra'ana also said obliquely, 'Then the world unnecessarily squanders its respect for the wives. From today I'm also one of your teeming subjects, not less, not more, eh?'

Liaqat very well knew that though he was the Prime Minister of Pakistan, at home he was just a husband. Therefore he said, 'No doubt you're my wife, and for me, that means the person who is closest to my heart. Only you rule there. But as for the country, it asserts its authority over every pore of my being. And you are not separate from this country. Anyway, a policy is going to be declared that will take Pakistan on the road of development and growth.'

'Oh, then…we'll wait…for that, wife will also wait who is so close to your heart. Do something that will join my heart also in the cheers of millions of common people and feel jubilant.'

She bid *adieu* to her husband with a smile. She was not aware that 16 October 1951 was going to bring tragedy for her—in the history of Pakistan, this date will be steeped in the blood which will spill over its fledgeling democratic foundation.

At precisely 11.30, Liaqat Ali Khan landed in the Viking plane of the Governor-General at Rawalpindi's Chaklala airbase. Among other engagements of the day, one was a mammoth meeting of the local Muslim League in Rawalpindi which he was scheduled to address at 4.00 in the afternoon. At the venue of the meeting at Company Bagh, about one lakh people had gathered to hear their fond leader. Slogans of 'Qaid-e-Millat' rent the air with a show of unusual enthusiasm. Liaqat felt gratitude for their display of respect and fondness for him. The podium was constructed as per his directive. He had given an order that the dais should be high and there should be only one chair: for him. He was, anyway, against all pompous exhibition of celebration. There was one more reason for keeping his podium plain and undecorated; he used to receive numerous letters complaining that common people found it difficult to have a look at him easily. That is why he ordered just one chair, a table and a mike.

The meeting commenced with the recitation of verses from the Holy Qur'an. There was a hushed silence of anticipation. The Chairman of Rawalpindi City Committee Masood Sadiq delivered his welcome speech. Then the Chief of the city Muslim League Sheikh Mohammad Umar addressed the meeting and welcomed the Prime Minister. When he invited the Prime Minister to deliver his speech, the crowd raised slogans cheering their leader.

Overwhelmed with this exuberance and full-throated enthusiasm, Liaqat Ali Khan got up straight. He had barely held the mike and uttered the words, 'Brethren of the nation…' when two shots rang out and terror gripped every heart. Before anyone could understand what was happening, Liaqat Ali Khan had collapsed face down. Despite it being an open area, no one could hear anything. Meanwhile, another explosive sound followed. The sequence was like this: Liaqat stood up, a round of applause, two words from Liaqat Ali Khan, then gunshots. The story was over!

The Prime Minister was shot dead. The silence of the graveyard could be heard. But soon pandemonium broke out.

'Madar-e-Millat has been assassinated.'

Such shouts rose and people ran helter-skelter. Soon after hearing the firing, policemen raised their guns and began firing in the air. Some people saw that one person had been nabbed and pinned down. He was thought to be the killer. Security men took hold of him. The angry mob also beat him up so badly that he died on the spot. Eyewitnesses reported that as soon as people saw him firing, they pounced on him to give him a big thrashing. He died then and there. Another version has it that some security officer shot him point-blank as soon as he was identified.

It appears that the so-called assassin was sitting in the front row facing the podium. The row was reserved for intelligence officers but he did not belong to the intelligence agency. Nor was he a worker or officer from any other department. How did he then occupy that seat remains a mystery to this day. His name was Saeed Akhtar and he was a citizen of Afghanistan. Sometime in the past, his father had given his life for the King of Afghanistan, Amanullah Khan. Saeed himself had served in the Afghan army, which he had deserted afterwards and sneaked into India. The British ruled here then and were kind enough to give him asylum in the country. Later on, he went to the North-West Frontier Province, now called Khyber Pakhtoonwa, and settled there. It is known that this assassin was a human bomb who had been a great admirer of Iqbal and Moulana Rumi. In January 1947, when the country was still under British rule, he requested political asylum in India which the government granted, and gave him and his family a home and a monthly allowance. Since then he had been living in Abbottabad.

When Liaqat Ali Khan was driven in Mushtaq Ahmed Gurmani's car to the Joint Military Hospital, he was unconscious. He was placed under the care of Dr Col Miyan and Dr Col Sarwar who tried hard to extract the bullets embedded in his body, but by then Liaqat had died.

A crowd of grieving, weeping people had gathered outside the hospital compound, all praying for the life of Liaqat Ali Khan, hoping against hope that there would be news of his survival. After a short while, Gurmani came out and waved to the mob, as though to say that all is well, no worry, he is alive. But then Dr Col Miyan joined him. He uttered only these words, 'My lips are sealed.'

Prime Minister Liaqat Ali Khan had passed away at 4.50 pm. A local news agency was the first to report that the assassin was a *Khaaqsaar* (lowly person). But soon afterwards this was withdrawn. Two hours later was released an official bulletin which mentioned him as the son of Babrak, a citizen of Afghanistan, belonging to the Zadran tribe of Khosht, Afghanistan who had been imprisoned under the Bengal Prohibitive Law 1818. His father was killed fighting on behalf of the Afghan king in a skirmish. Very few people had contact with the family as he was a supporter of Amanullah.

The then Chief of Army, General Ayub Khan writes in his biography:

> On hearing of the assassination of Liaqat Ali Khan when I reached there, I found that the new Prime Minister Khawaja Nazimuddin with his associates, Mohammad Ali, Mushtaq Ahmed and all others were deep in a jubilant mood. No one was taking Liaqat's name nor showing any grief. It seemed as though everyone was waiting for it. I thought they were all too selfish. They had no idea that the country had lost a man who had kept it united.

To investigate the assassination of Liaqat Ali Khan and the reasons behind it, an Enquiry Commission headed by Justice Muneer Ahmed Pakistan was set up on 1 November 1951. There were 38 sittings: 23 in Lahore and 15 in Rawalpindi. As many as 89 witnesses from the government and the public were examined and their statements recorded. At the end of all these exercises, three theories emerged. It was said that out of the three assumptions, two couldn't be made public because they involved national security. It would have endangered the interests of the nation to have published them. The Commission also took the angle that someone in a fit of religious intolerance murdered the Prime Minister; or someone who was displeased about Pakistan not declaring Jihad against India did it, alternatively, the deed was done as a result of mental instability of the perpetrator.

Eventually, after considering all aspects and points,

and examining witnesses, the Commission concluded that the killing did not take place in a mental fit of religious fanaticism, on the contrary, behind it was the possibility of a desire for a change of government. Liaqat Ali was the closest associate of Muhammad Ali Jinnah. It is true that later on there emerged some differences between them, nevertheless, the two had long been friends and had worked together. The Cold War between the US and the Soviet Union had started by the time Pakistan came into existence. Other countries of the world had to decide on which side they stood. America and Russia appeared to be competing for attracting large numbers of countries to their camps. Though Nehru was much impressed with the Soviet Union's trajectory of growth and performance, he declared that India would keep out of either of these camps and follow the middle path of non-alignment. Historical documents reveal that Jinnah favoured going along with the US but he didn't get much time to formulate Pakistan's policies. After his death, Liaqat came out as the strongest leader. Foreign policy took shape in his time, therefore it is said that Pakistan began to lean towards the US during his tenure. He was seen as an admirer of America. This is supposed to be one of the main reasons for Liaqat's murder.

It appeared that the country was rocked to its foundation with the death of first Jinnah in 1949 and then Liaqat Ali in 1951.

In 1949, the then US President Harry Truman invited Pandit Jawaharlal Nehru on a state visit. Liaqat was very displeased and took it as an insult. He didn't relish the US paying attention to India in such an appeasing manner. In those days, Gazanfar Ali Khan was Pakistan's Ambassador in Iran who had close, friendly contact with a Soviet diplomat. Gazanfar suggested to Liaqat that if the Americans are cultivating India's friendship, Pakistan should move closer to the Soviets. It is said that Liaqat had almost agreed to tour Moscow in response to an invitation he received once again. But US supporters in Pakistan's top bureaucracy were against it. At this point, Britain also began to share US anxiety over the matter. Its High Commissioner in Pakistan Sir Laurence Grafftey-Smith warned Foreign Minister Zafarullah Khan that it would not be possible for Britain and the US to ignore the developments if Liaqat went to Moscow. Caught in a peculiar dilemma, Liaqat cancelled his Russia tour. He had to get US funds so that Pakistan could proceed with its development projects. Some circles believed that though the visit was put off under American influence, he could no longer rely on America's assurances. He could not trust its politics. This is one reason, the theory goes, why the US Central Intelligence Agency thought it wise to remove Liaqat from its path.

Liaqat Ali Khan was born in the part of India that stayed in India after Partition. All Muslims like him who crossed over from India into Pakistan were called *muhajirs*. Those who had always stayed in the parts that became Pakistan did not have a good opinion about them. Liaqat is said to have a soft corner for them. He made sure that two per cent seats were reserved for *muhajirs* in Federal Civil Service vacancies while they formed only 1.5 per cent of the total population. Those who watched these developments closely affirm that the wealthy, traditionally powerful Muslims of Pakistan never liked these concessions, especially those living in Punjab who had considerable influence in Pakistan politics. Another line of thinking links it with Liaqat's killing.

It is also believed that Saeed Akhtar did not fire at all—it was somebody else and he had no reason to shoot the PM. He was not connected to politics in any way. There has to be some reason to have the guts to kill the Prime Minister of Pakistan in such a large, open-air public meeting. Taking into account these facts, it appears reasonable to say that Saeed was done to death unnecessarily. Alternatively, he was just a pawn in the hands of unseen forces that used him and then removed him from the scene instantly.

Some people think that the first *coup d'etat* was planned against the Liaqat government in 1949. He had become a *bête noire* for the army echelons and the top bureaucratic coterie. In their opinion, Pakistan couldn't capture the whole of Kashmir because of its administration. General Akbar Khan had masterminded this plot which came to be known as the 'Rawalpindi Conspiracy'. There were a dozen or so reliable associates. In February-March 1951, it was exposed. India's Governor-General Lord Mountbatten used to hold informal discussions with Pakistan Army General Douglas

Gracy. In one of his confidential reports, he wrote that Gracy endorsed his opinion that relations between the two countries had consistently been improving, except for the Kashmir issue! He also informed that India was transferring military hardware and equipment that were to be handed over to Pakistan and it was being done with appreciable honesty. The quantum of work was so great that in normal circumstances it would take at least three years to complete the task. But taking into account the communal skirmishes which created disruptions, such an operation might cover even five years. There should be no problem in accepting this though it would be in the interests of all to speed it up.

In a conversation which took place on 2 May 1948, Lord Mountbatten asked Gracy what would happen if a war flared up between India and Pakistan. Upon this Gracy responded that in that case, it would be useless for Pakistan to have any hope. Pakistan's Air Force is still incapable of going in the air and it would take many years for them to produce experts in the field. Their army might have been considered of greater calibre, but compared to the Indian Army it was just half in size and it stood no chance before India. Besides, it would certainly face scarcity of arms in a situation of war. Since Pakistan doesn't have any arms factory, it would be impossible to get a regular supply of armaments and ammunition. Anybody could guess that in a war-like situation, Pakistan could only look to a resounding defeat. Though it is believed that a Muslim soldier gives a tough fight to the last of his breath without bothering about death, that spirit is not enough to win a war.

Governor-General Mountbatten also wanted to know from General Gracy if the Pakistani ministers were aware of this. He observed that since the seat of the Central Government is in Karachi and the Military Headquarters is located in Rawalpindi, there was no regular and continuous contact between them, and on several occasions, their ministers had been told about it. The current political scenario easily led to the conclusion that the murder of Liaqat Ali Khan had been a political act, executed by those who wished to keep the government under their thumb, but who felt threatened by his manner of working and his policies. This has been analysed in detail in a research paper by Syed Muhammad Zulqarnain Zardi, a retired professor of a college in Islamabad. He propounded that the assassination had further eroded the already weak roots of Pakistan's democracy to such an extent that it would not recover from this setback.

The murder was a well-thought-out plot cleverly manipulated even to keep media confused, spreading all kinds of misinformation to the common masses. Thus minds were kept busy on a wrong track concerning the 16 October incident. Serious-minded people felt that the media by focusing on the assassination tried to deviate the mind of the people from the real issue, whereas all knew that the assassin was being made a scapegoat. It looks like he had no role in this high-profile drama. Then the mutually conflicting statements given by the government provoked the emotions of those who had understood the sequence of events with a degree of honesty.

Strangely enough, this sensational political killing found no place in two major newspapers of Pakistan, *Daily Imroze* and *Daily Zamindar* in their 17 October editions. No photographs were published in *Daily Pakistan* and *Daily Civil and Military Gazette* despite their journalists being present on the scene. *Pakistan Times* published three photos of Liaqat Ali Khan, but not a word concerning the assassination. This was taken in some quarters to be tantamount to an undeclared emergency by the information and broadcasting ministry.

Jinnah and Liaqat

The two individuals who are credited with laying the foundation of Pakistan are Muhammad Ali Jinnah and Liaqat Ali Khan. Both had great respect for one another. Although for some time they had a difference of opinion on certain issues, on the whole, they can be seen as a successful pair working in tandem.

Both of them possessed an intensity of passion that kept them motivated for working towards their goal of creating Pakistan but there was a difference in their respective family backgrounds and pattern of behaviour. Liaqat belonged to a reputable Nawab family—by today's standards, he could easily be classified in a multi-millionaire category that would make his life as luxurious and opulent as that of a princely state ruler.

That would make him so wealthy as to enable the next few generations' life equally luxurious, without needing to do anything. But his mettle was different. He was restive with a burning nationalist flame and wanted to see India as a fast-growing country. He had relinquished that family wealth and position in such a selfless mood that he handed over his Delhi bungalow for Pakistan's diplomatic mission. Not only this, he and Begum Ra'ana had also given up all their money and property before going to Pakistan. They vowed to lead a life of simplicity which is why she, despite being the late PM's widow, continued to live in a ramshackle, dilapidated house where she felt at ease. She was proud of her husband's humility and high thinking. It was found after Liaqat's death that his bank account contained only Rs 600 in savings which was then not sufficient to see the month through. Liaqat was a die-hard honest person, to the point of being stubborn—he never compromised with any of those standards which he had created. In the beginning, Begum Ra'ana felt a bit uncomfortable but by and by she adjusted to his system without difficulty. Once, officers of the Unclaimed Property Department requested Liaqat to put a claim to all those huge farms and fields and other property which he had left in Karnal and Muzaffarnagar. An angry Liaqat snubbed them with these words:

'Go! First attend to all those refugees' claim applications who have today neither a roof over their heads nor *roti* to eat. Complete that job first, and then you may come to me.'

Once Begum Ra'ana, finding an opportune time said, 'If you don't mind, we may make some arrangements in terms of property for our children's future.'

Liaqat replied, 'Begum… the whole of Pakistan is ours. Now, this is our home. The entire masses of people are our family—what more do you want?'

There is an important incident related to the property of Liaqat Ali Khan. India had sent a veteran leader Sri Prakash to Karachi as the first Indian Ambassador as he was on cordial terms with leaders in Pakistan. In his memoirs, he writes:

> Mrs Liaqat Ali Khan sought my favour in the matter of property left in India *(read Muzaffarnagar)*. I succeeded in getting the matter resolved though I had to take the PM J L Nehru in confidence on this matter. I got the message from New Delhi in this regard. Incidentally, I happened to meet Liaqat Ali Khan and communicated the same to him. He was displeased and muttered words that his wife should not have taken up the matter with the Indian authorities. I was taken aback as I was under the impression that Begum Liaqat had taken her husband in confidence. On the other hand, Jinnah used to pester me often about his bungalow in Bombay. He was so eager about his property in Bombay that he even told me to take up the matter on a personal level with Nehru.

That was the difference. Liaqat's son Ashraf was sent

to Lahore's Atkinson College where the children of only princely families used to be admitted. When Ashraf came home for vacation, he took time to unlock his heart to his father, 'Dad, I feel so bad when I see that all the children are accompanied by their attendants and servants who take care of every single requirement of theirs. And here I am, going and coming all alone, nobody to attend to my needs.'

Liaqat remarked, 'If you're so fond of servants and attendants, leave your school and come back home, you'll find plenty of them here.'

Ashraf remained silent, which was taken to be his consent. He was withdrawn from the college in Lahore and sent to an ordinary school in Karachi. Today it sounds incredible that a man who had an abundance of wealth, who was the Prime Minister of Pakistan and who could have led a life of luxury, chose to live like a common man. After death, when his shoes were removed, his socks were found to be full of holes.

With the making of Pakistan, an endless string of problems loomed before him, but there was no sign of perturbation either on the face of Liaqat Ali Khan or that of Begum Ra'ana. There were also certain attributes in his personality which put a question mark on his image. He disliked opposition to such an extent that when he used to talk about his opponents, he often stooped to a disconcertingly low level. Liaqat's verbal assaults were straightforward but full of objectionable charges, filthy and unbearable.

In this connection, Allen Mac Grath writes in his book, *The Destruction of Pakistan's Democracy:*

> Liaqat had direct and powerful ideas about party politics. Those who formed other parties were called traitors, false and vain. When he talked about the opposition, his language stooped to such a level as to spout expressions like 'Indian dogs'. From his point of view, to oppose the Muslim League was equal to going against Pakistan. However one tries, it is not possible to gather much information about Liaqat Ali Khan. Praising him frequently, a writer feels, 'He was a person who was born in wealth and prosperity, yet despite having everything, died in poverty. There was a great difference in the style of his and Jinnah's working'. It can be said, 'Jinnah was certainly a great leader of his time, but Liaqat Ali Khan was a far better human being.'

Fatima and Ra'ana

Few people know that in May 1939, Muhammad Ali Jinnah had nominated his sister Fatima and Liaqat Ali Khan as trustees of his property in his last will. After that, Jinnah survived for nine years but there was no change in his will, which suggests that he had a deep faith in Liaqat. This is reflected in an incident which occurred in Liaqat's home 'Gul-e-Ra'ana'. It was a regular habit of Jinnah and Fatima to visit Liaqat's house and spend time playing cards. Once at the end of a round of the game, Liaqat casually referred to Jinnah's lonesome life and suggested that he must consider remarrying. With a smile on his face, he looked at Ra'ana and said, 'Yes, I must surely marry, if I get another Ra'ana!'

When Pakistan came into being, Jinnah's health had

considerably declined. By the time he shifted to Karachi he had grown very weak and was sick a great deal of the time. His sister Fatima gave up her work in Bombay as a dentist and went to Karachi to live full time with him. She kept close to him like a shadow. She was very worried about him. Many didn't like this, unfortunately. Among such people were Liaqat and Begum Ra'ana. Once Fatima complained to her brother about the Begum's behaviour towards her.

It was just a minor incident. In 1947, after the formation of Pakistan, the Governor of Sindh invited Muhammad Ali Jinnah and Fatima to an official banquet. Begum Ra'ana was asked to take the chair near Fatima, which she declined saying, 'Other people should also get a chance.'

Fatima didn't like this remark and drew Jinnah's attention to it later on. But Jinnah was Jinnah. He knew how to create a balance. So he did not show any immediate reaction.

Begum Ra'ana's birthday fell on 25 December. That year her birthday was being celebrated in free Pakistan. Guests had begun coming. Jinnah too came along with Fatima; he complimented Ra'ana thus:

'Whatever anyone says…you are wonderful! All others fade away before you… Impossibly wonderful….!'

The comments drew uproarious laughter from everyone present. This had been said many times among high diplomats and elite guests. But that day it was completely out of place, and Begum Ra'ana was grinding her teeth in exasperation. When all guests had left, the Begum was still disturbed. She had great respect for Jinnah. Such talk was not expected from him. Husband and wife gave a good deal of thought to it and agreed that it showed bad manners. Liaqat had boundless love for his wife. The couple had matured in their emotional tuning and felt mutually fulfilled. The Begum could not get over this incident. Then Liaqat took a step which Jinnah must never have imagined. In a brief letter written to Muhammad Ali Jinnah, Liaqat Ali Khan submitted his resignation from the post of Prime Minister. He wrote it in very harsh words.

When Jinnah received the letter, he felt very bad about it. He refused to consider the resignation because he felt that there existed not just a political understanding between them but they were bound by a strong friendship. Later on, Jinnah realised the seriousness of his jocular remarks which became such an issue. Though his intention was not what was being made out, the impression it left did not portend well for anyone.

Despite this, Liaqat firmly stated that the remark directed at his wife did not permit him to continue as the Prime Minister. After several discussions and efforts to dispel the misunderstanding, Jinnah requested Liaqat to bring the matter to an end. He also said, 'Let us promise each other that any debate between Ra'ana Begum and Fatima will not be the cause of personal misunderstanding between us.'

He also made it clear that his attitude to Ra'ana had

been that of an affectionate father.

Quite different from these accounts is another assumption which seeks to establish that Begum Ra'ana was deeply fascinated and enchanted with Jinnah. Once she said that when she first saw Jinnah, he struck the deepest chord in her heart. 'At first he appears to be a proud and self-opinionated person, but if you meet him after that you understand what deep springs of profound feelings are hidden in him!'

It may be considered good luck for Pakistan that the entire controversy resolved itself without unusual scenes and no one besides them came to know about it. Had it been allowed to grow out of proportion, no one can tell what disagreeable results it would have borne for Pakistan's political milieu. Nonetheless, Fatima and Ra'ana were never comfortable with each other, nor did tensions ease after the death of Jinnah and Liaqat. On many occasions, Fatima used to observe directly and indirectly that Liaqat tried to cheat Jinnah many a time, and also that the Liaqat-Desai Pact had created unrelieved tensions between them which continued till Jinnah's death.

In this connection, another dispute had caught people's attention. On 30 December 1947, Pakistan's cabinet passed an important resolution underlining that no policy decision will be deemed as approved unless that cabinet meeting is chaired by Jinnah. In the event of a dispute or difference between Jinnah and Liaqat, Jinnah's decision would apply. That shows that not all was fine between the two giants of Pakistan politics. One fundamental distinction between them was that Jinnah to a great extent was materialistic by temperament. He showed to others strong adherence to Islamic principles but in truth, his love for the Western style of life was manifested everywhere. He sold his majestic bungalow at 10, Aurangzeb Road, Delhi at a considerably high price. He had another large house in Bombay which he didn't know what to do with. Since he had become a Pakistani, as per law his bungalow was termed evacuee property and came under the ownership of the Government of India. In those days, such buildings were used for government offices. Jinnah had personally written to the Indian Prime Minister Jawaharlal Nehru to conserve it. Nehru accepted his request. But later on, as the tension between the two countries increased, Nehru told Jinnah to find a suitable tenant for his house as it was not possible for him to continue to take care of it indefinitely.

After Liaqat

For Ra'ana Begum, the death of Liaqat was an unbearable, heart-breaking stroke of misfortune. But she had herself chosen the path along which lay unseen dangers and Liaqat became a martyr on that very path. She did not turn away from that path herself nor did she waver from fulfilling her responsibilities. On the contrary now she was in the grip of a new passion which propelled her onwards to risk many dangers to fulfil her husband's dreams. She faced unanticipated challenges at every step in a land where she was not yet established. Many occasions came when her métier was tested and she had to pass through stages of depression. But she revived her spirits and didn't allow herself to be overwhelmed, with the result that many doors opened before her that took her to greater heights.

The way she gathered herself with admirable poise, facing dark hours with a composed face after Liaqat's gruesome murder and put herself in the service of the country was incredible. One wonders where all that spiritual stamina came from. She showed that she was not a weak, dispirited doll—she looked forward to building a nation of strong, self-reliant women, launching organized programmes for their proper education and training that would make them socially useful. She zealously embarked upon the long-term plan of bringing Pakistani women in the mainstream of life. A radical transformation in these women was being brought about by Begum Ra'ana, who opened their minds to the true sense of dignity of living and showed how that life could be made meaningful. She also told them about their rights and duties.

Liaqat's Begum had, to some extent, imbibed his temperament, having lived with him for such a long time.

On 17 October 1951, that is, the day after the catastrophe, Begum Ra'ana was scheduled to inaugurate a hospital in Karachi. She couldn't go there as she was in mourning but a message was sent with the direction that the programme need not be postponed. She sent a recorded message in which she observed, 'When Allah gives us, He has the right to take things away from us. That's His way for us. It's because of this divine service which we receive that we get the strength to rise above common personal interests and sorrows and think about making progress in life. With these feelings, I'm making a humble beginning by declaring the opening of the

Seventh Day Adventist Hospital.'

It must have taken a superhuman effort for her to remain normal. Her husband had been killed barely twenty-four hours before. She not only controlled her emotions but having resumed normal life, stepped out to serve her country, fearlessly and stoically.

A great crisis seems to have overtaken the new-born country, still grappling with unforeseen problems and trying to get its bearings. Removal of its singularly gifted leader created a new situation not easy to handle. Ra'ana decided to put everything she had into realising her husband's dreams, and more importantly, paving the way to lead its people along the road of development. Liaqat's close friend Yusuf Harun said:

> Those who knew him since long years are amazed at how that man, not caring at all for money, his comfort and time, took the Muslim League along with him to build a new Pakistan. Liaqat and his family have transformed themselves into the Islamic idea of plain living. Abandoning the big bungalow with spacious, beautiful marble halls, big rooms and endless seeming banquet halls, they took up a dilapidated and uncomfortable looking house as their official residence. In the verandah was their dressing room in one corner...Once I spotted him shaving in that dressing room and told him that he might catch a cold in a place like this. To this, he replied in that characteristic manner for which he was famous, 'Thank Allah! I've at least

a roof over my head. What about those countless people who do not have even that?

Barely two days before his murder, Liaqat Ali Khan had remarked in his speech in Karachi, 'I'm not wealthy. I do not have property. And I'm happy that I do not have these things, because they weaken a person's faith. I've only my life and the mission that I must remain dedicated to Pakistan. Besides I can see that even when I am called on to spill my blood for the defence of Pakistan, the blood of Liaqat is always ready.'

Not one but many problems confronted Liaqat Ali. The country's army could not be depended on; its higher officers were not in agreement with the Prime Minister over his diplomatic policy concerning India. They regarded his efforts to consolidate the country's democratic and federal structure with a lot of suspicion. Also, he was not comfortable with the Chief of Pakistan Army General Gracy Douglas. Finally, in January 1951 this Army Chief of foreign origin tendered his resignation. General Ayub Khan was nominated the first indigenous Chief of Army Staff, Commander-in-Chief of Pakistan.

Posthumously, Liaqat Ali Khan was conferred the title of 'Shahid-e-Millat' or 'Nation's Martyr'. He was buried in the mausoleum 'Qaid-e-Millat', now known as Liaqat Bagh. Begum Ra'ana's children were very young, fourteen and eleven years old, and were deprived of their father's protective umbrella. Their mother had the twin task of giving them proper attention and working for all those projects which remained unfinished due to Liaqat's death. It was a Herculean task. People thought that with the disappearance of Liaqat, Begum Ra'ana would also go into oblivion. But she had learned a lot from his strong character, his ideals and values had become her standard too. She was prepared to tackle new challenges and old problems with renewed energy and resolve. Liaqat's dreams of a new strong Pakistan were beholden to Begum Ra'ana's courageous spirit and tireless efforts.

Many people conjectured that after Liaqat's exit his wife would go to India, lay her legal claim on his paternal property and settle down there for the rest of her life in the glow of wealth and luxury. Contrary to this speculation, she wanted to be a role model for Pakistani women and such thoughts never entered her head. Although severe economic problems had suddenly arisen and began to nag her, she decided to stand up to this new crisis and carve a place for herself in history. She appealed to the Pakistan government, which gave her a house at Lahore's Moti Manaz. But she sold that house and purchased another in Karachi. Around this time came forward a family friend of theirs named Jamshed Markar who gave her a blank cheque, saying that he very well knew the real financial position of late Liaqat Ali Khan. He also knew that being a lady of great self-respect she wouldn't accept any monetary help.

Begum Ra'ana had acquired great insight and tactical skill in politics by now, like a seasoned player, thanks to her husband who had taken her under his care and tutelage. Besides she had created her special place in the public domain as an economist and an interested social activist whose efforts centred on raising women's standards of living. We have already seen how significant her association with her husband was in creating Pakistan. In the brief sequel to independence, her work for women had set the pace for the country's forward march which unfortunately got disrupted due to Liaqat's demise.

Now she took the reins in her hands for the second innings.

Ra'ana had begun in the newly free Pakistan the self-appointed task to bring out women to give them vocational training and explore employment opportunities for them. But soon she realised that this was not enough; there was a need to expand the range of efforts. For this she required committed women volunteers, ready to dedicate themselves for it. One such organisation under her leadership was the All Pakistan Women's Association whose first convention was called at her official residence at Karachi in 1949. She might have been inspired to set up such an organisation by observing the effective role played by similar national-level organisations in India and China. She had been advised by Begum Jahanara Shanawaz also to mobilise women's organisations on the pattern of All India Women's Conference, which was doing impressive work in India. Begum Ra'ana gave Jahanara the responsibility to frame the constitution of the association, and also nominated her as its Senior Vice-Chairperson. She was its founder Chairperson and looked after it till the end. The main aim of this body was to raise the social, educational, cultural and political status of women. It was hoped that it would become a representative organisation of Pakistani women and was considered eligible to function as a social and economic advisory body to the United Nations.

Though Liaqat's death had tragically transformed Begum Ra'ana's life, she didn't allow its gloom to affect her activities. On the contrary, she plunged with greater vigour into her organisation, accepting the severe challenges of a new life of bereavement and was glad to see Muslim women come out of their homes to make many notable achievements on the international scene. The organisation became a medium to propel the country's women force into several developmental projects. This is her legacy to Pakistan's conservative society for which she is remembered as a relentless crusader. She also played a decisive role in the initial years in the Constituent Assembly for reserving seats for women. In that early phase, there was a wonderful expansion of this organisation in the country. In 1951, it emerged as the finest organisation in Pakistan and had a shining image in the public mind. Its roots had spread in the adjacent rural areas as well as on the state level. Workshops for women were set up in most of the major cities and towns and sale outlets were established for exhibiting and selling products which were manufactured in them.

Diplomacy and Empowerment

Immediately after Pakistan was born, she made great efforts to set up an organisation called Pakistani Women's Volunteer Service as a vehicle for improving the quality and level of women's activities and went on updating the mechanism of coordination. This was that difficult period in people's lives when women who had never stepped out of their homes offered help to the dislocated and homeless and were forced to stay at refugee camps or in hospitals and roadside camps. This campaign was supervised by Begum Ra'ana. It was this tireless endeavour that made the government turn its attention to women's issues, create special offices and departments and speed up the process of giving help to the affected masses. Lost and Found offices were set up along with employment bureau, marriage bureau, widow centre, rehabilitation homes for abducted women, and so on, which were efficiently run by volunteers. Begum Ra'ana took a personal interest in running camps and used to visit destitute women to assess their needs and supply the required items and services.

In those trying times, she went out of her way to provide essential goods to the remotest areas of the city where access to these goods was difficult. She arranged for vehicles and kept a watch over the supply line. She paid particular attention to those who were not in a position to move out and saw that they were supplied blankets, clothes, food and other necessary articles. After Partition, with the number of refugees swelling everywhere, health problems had aggravated to such an extent that urgent steps were necessary. The situation required methodical handling and thus Begum Ra'ana arranged resources for urgent measures to be taken. As the situation showed some improvement, the need was felt for establishing a special women's armed wing. With this in view, in January 1948, the Pakistan's Women's National Guard was set up where special military training was imparted to women.

In addition, she founded the Pakistan Women's Nursing Reserve in Karachi in 1948, in which focus was on nursing and first aid. It was a noble step, for in Muslim families before Partition, it was unthinkable for women to come out of their homes and adopt nursing as a profession. Ra'ana took the revolutionary step of approaching orthodox families to open their doors to allow women to channelise their talents for socially meaningful work. Her mission received a fair amount of success. A few select candidates were sent to foreign universities, including London, for specialised training. Trainers from overseas were invited to impart modern training to local women, a step which proved most useful.

Despite adverse conditions prevailing in the society, Begum Ra'ana desired to build a strong structure in the newly formed country in the field of women's education. With this in view, she first lobbied the government to establish in Karachi the Ra'ana Liaqat Ali Khan College and then in Lahore the Home Economics College. From childhood, when she used to accompany her mother, she had nurtured the fond hope of doing something radical for women's development. Now when the changed circumstances opened a broader area before her, she decided to contribute her best to the cause and transform her ideas into reality.

As an economist, Ra'ana Begum understood what was needed to improve the productivity of labourers working in small-scale units and how their health and lifestyle problems demand special attention. She took particular interest in these issues. Taking into account the need to improve and promote arts and crafts which lay scattered and unorganised, she took the initiative to set up Pakistan Cottage Industries Association in 1948. To a great extent, this Association was successful in creating wide interest in local artware and exploring the market for handicrafts.

This singular effort eased the problem of finding finances and generating employment for many who were on the verge of starvation. Millions of dislocated refugees found stability and direction in their lives. Such a move not only gave them a respectful status in life but raised their standard of living. With these encouraging successes, Ra'ana Begum's mind became busier visualising new areas to be charted and explored. Soon she came up with the idea of Ra'ana Liaqat Craftsman Colony and Pakistan Cottage Industries Emporium. For the settlement of refugees, she established in Karachi the Gul-e-Rana Nusrat Industrial Home where refugee women got decent employment and good wages and salaries apart from yearly incentives of handsome amounts.

In February 1949, Begum Ra'ana convened a meeting of the All Pakistan Women's Conference at the residence of the Prime Minister. About 150 women who had achieved distinction at the national level in different fields of work participated in it. Later, she chose a few active women of the society to form All Pakistan Women's Association. This emerged as a powerful organisation whose list of notable works is quite long. Even today, it is actively engaged in working for the all-round growth and improvement of women. A special feature of it is that she kept it away from party politics and the complications such involvement creates. From those days till today, this body is known by its attainments and efforts. Its branches have spread to every district and province of the country with women in thousands registered as members. Besides its two major branches, there are 62 other branches. UNICEF accreditation has categorised it as a Grade B advisory body. It is also at par with world-class women's organisations such as the General Federation of Women's Club, International Alliance of Women, The Associated Country Women of the World, International Council of the World and the World Assembly of the Youth. It invariably becomes part of the activities of these world organisations. It has an important share of official posts and committees in workshops, lectures, discussions, international delegations and deputations as well as advisory bodies. This Pakistan Women's Organisation has proved its importance and value in promoting Pakistani women, improving their general awareness and empowering them by extending its reach to the grassroot level in rural areas by organising national programmes, training workshops and social and legal activities.

This can be best understood if we take into account the socio-cultural reality of Muslim women of this geographical region before Partition. The world outside the four walls of the home was denied to them. For centuries, the women used to lead a confined life of isolation, they were neither found fit to impart any useful information nor supposed to get involved in any social activities. If any woman tried to break out of these restrictions and participate in social events, a lot of hue and cry was raised in society, newspapers and magazines. She had to face all kinds of nasty accusations and discouragements.

An illustration will throw sufficient light on this dark side of a woman's place. By the 1940s, the Muslim League had a few women members also. In April of that year, burqa-clad women took out a procession condemning a ban on an organisation called Khaqsaar Tahreeq and arrest of certain leaders of the Muslim League. This was the first organised attempt of Muslim women of those days—one newspaper commented that these were 'shameless women' and portrayed them as bent upon destroying the idea of Pakistan. Also, this was the first time when a women's procession was sought to be sabotaged and many of them were arrested. No doubt, it was a formidable task to enlighten Muslim women whose background had been heavily laden with orthodox thinking and non-liberal practices. The issue became one of greater struggle when one considers that the Begum herself came from a different cultural background. Yet it was the humane and liberal side of her social mission which prompted her to stir up a general movement for the good of wider sections of Muslim women. This is what makes Begum Ra'ana the foremost leader of the Women's Empowerment Movement. She was then considered the First Lady of Pakistan.

The two major organisations which Ra'ana Begum had built up represented the difficult work she had undertaken to stand up against the orthodox values which idealised male authority and strengthened gender disparity of all kinds. Government machinery had given its support to the Pakistan Women Naval Reserve and

Pakistan Women's National Guard. They came directly under army and navy and were formed with the possibility that there may be a war with India. However, she was their chief controller and had the freedom of regulating its influence and functioning.

When under her direction training in signalling, coding, use of firearms and knowledge of defence technique began to be imparted, different sections of society protested strongly against women's entry into the army. Begum Ra'ana had to add a *dupatta* (scarf) to the women's dress to maintain a balance. However, patriarchal dissatisfaction and complaints were not quite silenced. Women's entry into what had for centuries been considered an exclusively male bastion was looked upon with suspicion and hostility. Moreover, Liaqat Ali Khan's assassination had weakened his Begum's position. It is said that the government devised a new way to render the organisation weaker. Ra'ana Begum was appointed ambassador to the Netherlands—in her absence, the associations she nurtured became dormant.

The yardsticks which Ra'ana Begum had formulated while establishing her women's organisations admitted women above seventeen years irrespective of caste, colour, community, faith or religion. Its object was to strengthen the feelings of compassion and humane service in women. These bodies also aimed at guaranteeing women's greater participation in social, cultural, educational and political life by raising and enriching their consciousness and making their life purposeful in the mission of nation-building. A notable feature of this campaign was that women from the poorest and the weakest to the middle class to the richest strata were drawn in. Begum Ra'ana tried to cover every aspect of women's life—economic, health and employment problems were particularly attended to. Several schools, health centres and industrial units were opened. For income generation, sewing, weaving and such activities were promoted, which helped them in a big way. Although the movement was in its infancy and most of the centres were located in major cities like Lahore, Karachi, Peshawar and other district headquarters, their benefits had no doubt started reaching every such woman who needed them.

The organisation which was known as APWA worked in coordination with the Pakistan government in the early years. Regular funding and protection from the government made it possible for it to work efficiently. Besides, politicians had no problem with it since it didn't indulge in politics and had exclusively focused on development and welfare plans for women. Nevertheless, Begum Ra'ana intelligently went on expanding the scope of this seminal women's organisation and brought into its purview a little bit of political and legal interest as well.

In 1953, APWA passed a resolution demanding 10 per cent reservation for women's representation in state and national assemblies. Religious clerics and dogmatic elements soon began to target the Begum and her activities for various reasons, especially for not wearing *hijab* or *purdah*. Assault on character and morality is the easiest way of countering and disrupting such progressive campaigns. One such right-wing conservative organisation, Majlis-e-Ahrar began a slur campaign against Begum Ra'ana and other women leaders by calling them 'call girls'. Jamat-e-Islami and Jamayat-ul-Ulema-e-Islam also did not accept her. They had actively been engaged in spreading venom against these women's efforts in making a new and strong Pakistan. Various camps of religious fundamentalism have since ancient days been active against the idea of women's freedom of choice and speech, but in those early years they began to be menacingly outspoken and aggressive.

Begum Ra'ana, however, had become a dauntless crusader for the cause of Pakistan's development, especially its women. To achieve this, she set up many other organisations besides the ones mentioned above. In this chain, she established Karachi Business and Professional Women's Club which opened opportunities for women of diverse professions to gather on a platform and seek a solution to their problems through discussion and debate. Branches of this Club were opened in Lahore, Peshawar and Rawalpindi.

Federation of University Women was set up in 1956, which offered big moral support to aspirant women craving to do something worthwhile in life. Begum Ra'ana's presence gave them plenty of morale-boosting assurance. It became a significant channel for offering job opportunities to educated women. After her husband's death, she maintained a discreet distance from politics and concentrated on social welfare. She had stirred interest among diplomatic circles. She owed the distinction of becoming the first woman leader of the delegation to be sent by the Pakistan government to the UN in 1952. Queen Elizabeth II of England invited her to the coronation ceremony the very next year.

She happened to be the only woman delegate in the group of Commonwealth members to attend the Queen's coronation. It was a great mark of her achievements that she became the first woman Ambassador of Pakistan to the Netherlands, in which capacity she continued till 1961. Soon she came to be known as a capable top-ranking statesperson in diplomatic circles. Later, she was appointed Ambassador to Italy, where she remained posted till 1965. The same year, she was sent to Tunisia and continued in office till 1966.

Though during these years she was mostly out of the country, her interest in matters concerning women of Pakistan did not in any way become slack. It was due to pressure exerted by her that in 1961, the Muslim Family Ordinance was presented for bringing about changes in Islamic Marriage Law. This heralded a radical change in the direction of growth in the patriarchal and excessively conservative society of Pakistan. On 2 March 1961, then Field Marshal Ayub Khan passed the ordinance with some amendments, making it a law. The next year, the Women's Association conducted an extensive survey of the usefulness and deficiencies of this law. Based upon this survey, she suggested certain improvements which included setting up of family courts. The law was implemented in the country in 1964.

In 1967, Begum Ra'ana returned to her country and took up the post of Professor in the Government College of Home Economics where she worked till 1973. She was also bestowed with the honorary degree of Doctor of Philosophy in Economics by the Government College University.

After coming under the influence of Pakistan Peoples' Party under Chairman Zulfiqar Ali Bhutto, she joined the party in 1970 but didn't become active for the next two years. In 1972, when Pakistan was going through a difficult crisis and had lost its eastern wing, Begum Ra'ana, at the call of Bhutto, became active in political movements. She also accepted a ministerial post in his government where she was assigned the charge of Minister of Economics and Finance. She took many decisions of national importance which had a long-term impact. Bhutto encouraged her to take part in the forthcoming elections in which she won handsomely.

She was appointed Governor of Sindh Province, thus becoming the first woman governor of a province, which meant that she also became the Chancellor of Sindh and Karachi Universities. Begum Ra'ana continued in her office till 1976 when Parliamentary elections were declared. She participated in them and won, but due to a state of martial law imposed by Pakistan Chief of Army Staff General Zia- ul-Haq, she could not take the oath.

She was the lone woman politician who not only openly defied martial law but registered strong protest against the excesses being perpetrated against Zulfiqar Ali Bhutto and publicly deplored the vindictive politics which led the authorities to hang him finally. When Bhutto was sentenced to death, she shed profuse tears for this tragedy for four days. She launched such a protest campaign against Zia-ul-Haq that it appeared for a time that the authorities would not withstand it. She mobilised a formidable mass movement against the military rule but considering her high and respectful position in the country's politics, the Zia administration couldn't muster enough courage to take action against her. Despite her advanced years and a few age-related ailments, the Begum not only led the protest against the cruel military regime of Zia-ul-Haq and the execution of Bhutto, but called the Islamic laws imposed in Pakistan as anti-Constitutional, rallied educated people and motivated them to stand up against them. She said that these Islamic laws not only go against the Constitution of the country but negate the true spirit of Islam and act against granting women a respectable status in society.

Begum Ra'ana was Pakistan's most respected, popular and educated stateswoman. For decades, no other woman like her appeared on the scene, at least until Benazir Bhutto became Prime Minister (for two terms, 1988-90 and 1993-96). Hers was a well-rounded personality and she always came well prepared for discussions. She understood the subjects and issues perfectly, leading whatever struggle she deemed necessary with exemplary honesty and integrity.

The UN conferred on her a special award in 1978, honouring her for her relentless fight for making efforts to improve women's condition in Pakistan. The title of 'Maadar-e-Pakistan' was already given to her in 1950 while her husband lived. In 1959, 'Nishan-e-Pakistan' was conferred on her which is the highest civilian award given to distinguished persons. After Pakistan became a Republic, Turkey honoured her with the country's top prestigious award for being a great woman leader. Similarly, Italy and the Netherlands also gave her their country's top honours.

Begum Ra'ana passed away on 13 June 1990 and was buried beside her husband in Karachi's Qaid-e-Azam mausoleum. Her death stamped her name indelibly on the pages of her country's history. The woman who was born in India in a Hindu family which had adopted Christianity, who later got converted to Islam, became an integral part of her country's turbulent history. She still shines on its pages for her unparalleled feats and achievements. Her sacrifices and inexorable strivings for building a country for the Muslims of the sub-continent while working alongside her husband can never be forgotten.

A special postage stamp of one rupee was issued by the Pakistan Government in her honour on 14 August 1991 which was conceptualised and designed by Professor Said Akhtar of Lahore's National College of Arts. On her birth centenary in 2005, another stamp of four rupees was released.

Appendix

Begum Ra'ana's elder son Ashraf Liaqat Ali Khan was born in Shimla in 1937. When his parents shifted to Karachi, Ashraf was studying in a Delhi school. He was admitted to Atkinson College, Karachi from where he completed his high school education. After that, he was sent to England's Rugby School for studies in Technology and Arts. He also studied in England's Belmont Preparatory School and afterwards in Mill Hill School. He also studied Law in England's King's College.

Ashraf was just fourteen years old when his father Liaqat Ali Khan was assassinated. He worked for Rugby's English Electric Company and from 1959 to 1962 with the Dutch Airlines KLM in Rotterdam. From 1980 to 2004, he was associated with Ashraf Eastern Travels. It is during this period that his mother Begum Ra'ana died.

He made an attempt to enter mainstream politics which was not successful. Ashraf joined the political party Tahreek-e-Istaqbal launched by the retired Air Marshal Asghar Khan and contested National Assembly elections from Mirpur Khas but failed to win.

His younger brother Akbar Liaqat Ali Khan too tried his luck in an election in 1970. He was given a ticket from Liaqatabad seat but his opponent, a Jamat-e-Islami candidate, defeated him. After these defeats, both the brothers decided to quit politics.

Akbar looked after his trading business while staying in Karachi. Besides, he was also associated with the airlines and tourism business. Ashraf remained President of the Sindh Club from 2006 to 2008. It was during this period that lung cancer was detected and he died on 28 July 2014, leaving behind his wife, two sons and a daughter.

References

Abdullah, Faisal, 'Women of Pakistan: Begum Ra'ana Liaqat Ali Khan', *Jazbah* magazine, 2008.

Agarwal, Deepa, *The Begum: A Portrait of Ra'ana Liaqat Ali Khan, Pakistan's Pioneering First Lady*, Penguin Viking, 2019.

All Pakistan Woman Association, *Kumaoni People,* APWA Public Press, Directorate for Public Services.

All Pakistan Women's Association, *Ra'ana Liaqat Ali Khan; Biography and Speeches*, Karachi, 2007.

Azmat, Hina, 'Rethinking of Begum Ra'ana Liaqat Ali

Khan's Services for Women Empowerment', *Journal of Punjab University Historical Society*, Vol. 32, Issue 1, Jan-June 2019.

Bhatnagar, Rajendra Mohan, *Ruttie Jinnah* (Hindi), Harper Hindi, 2016.

Hicks, Pamela, *Daughter of Empire;* a source of inspiration for the film *Viceroy's House*, W&N, 2017.

Joshi, Sanjay, 'Juliet Got It Wrong: Names and identities among Christian Converts of Kumaon, 1850-1930', *Journal of Asian Studies,* Vol 74., No 4 (Nov 2015).

Kazim, Muhammad Reza, *Liaqat Ali Khan: His Life and Works*, OUP Pakistan, 2003.

Masroor, Mehr Nigar, *Ra'ana Liaqat Ali Khan, A Biography*, All Pakistan Women's Association, Karachi, 1980.

Miles, Kay, *The Dynamo in Silk*, All Pakistan Women's Association, Karachi, 1974.

Pande, Ira, *Diddi* (Hindi), Penguin India, 2009.

Pande, Nilima, *Lucknow Shahar, Kuchh Dekha—Kuchh Suna* (Hindi), Bodhi Prakashan, Jaipur, 2019.

Long, Roger D., *Dear Mr Jinnah*, OUP, 2005.

McGarth, Allen, *The Destruction of Pakistan's Democracy*, OUP, Karachi, 1996.

Mukherjee, Madhushree, *Churchill's Secret War; The British Empire and the Ravaging of India During World War II*, Penguin, 2018.

Pirbhai, M. Reza, *Fatima Jinnah: Mother of the Nation*, Cambridge University Press, 2017.

Reddy, Sheela, *Mister and Misses Jinnah* (Hindi) transl. by Madan Soni, Manjul Publishing House, 2019.

Shamsie, Muneeza, 'Life Devoted to Human Welfare', *The Dawn*, 11 June 1982.

Soigal, Rubina, *Feminism and the Women's Movement in Pakistan: Actors, Debates and Strategies*, A Country Study, 2016.

Talwalkar, Govind, *Sattantar 1947,* (Hindi) Part 1-3, transl. by Ravindra Dattatreya Telang, Samvad Prakashan, Meerut, 1st ed., 2019.

Tunzelmann, Alex von, *Indian Summer: The Secret History of the End of an Empire*, Simon and Schuster, UK, 2008.

Websites

https://www.ecyclopedia.com/women/encyclopedias-almanacs-transcripts-and-maps/khan-begum-liaqat-ali-1905-1990

https://en.wikipedia.org/wiki/Ra'ana_Liaquat_Ali_Khan

https://historypak.com/raana-liaquat-ali-khan/

https://www.dawn.com/news/1122254

https://en.wikipedia.org/wiki/Liaquat_Ali_Khan